GOVERNMENT VERSUS TRADE UNIONISM IN BRITISH POLITICS SINCE 1968

Government versus Trade Unionism in British Politics since 1968

Gerald A. Dorfman

HOOVER INSTITUTION PRESS
STANFORD UNIVERSITY STANFORD, CALIFORNIA

HOOVER INSTITUTIONS PRESS
STANFORD CALIFORNIA

© Gerald A. Dorfman 1979

First published 1979 by
THE MACMILLAN PRESS LTD
London and Basingstoke
Delhi Dublin
Hong Kong Johannesburg Lagos
Melbourne New York Singapore Tokyo

Hoover Institution Publication 224

The Hoover Institution on War, Revolution and Peace, founded at Stanford University in 1919 by the late President Herbert Hoover, is an interdisciplinary research center on domestic and international public affairs in the twentieth century. The views expressed in its publications are entirely those of the authors and do not necessarily reflect the views of the staff, officers, or Board of Overseers of the Hoover Institution.

Library of Congress Catalog card No. 78–70886

ISBN: 0-8179-7241-2

Contents

Acknowledgements

I wrote this book while a National Fellow at the Hoover Institution at Stanford University. I am grateful to Hoover for its generous support and to Dennis Bark, the Executive Secretary of the National Fellow Program. Agnes Peterson, Curator of the West European collection at Hoover and her assistant, Helen Berman, were especially helpful and very kind to me during my year in residence. Senior Fellows Peter Duignan and Lewis Gann took a strong interest in my work and I wish to express my gratitude to them.

I did all of the research for this project in Britain. The Trades Union Congress generously provided me with access to its library during my many stays in London between 1969 and 1977. I am also very grateful to the dozens of political and union leaders, members of the TUC staff, and civil servants who so generously participated in long interviews with me. Lord Allen, Lord Greene, and George Woodcock were especially kind on a number of occasions over several years.

Professor Victor Olorunsola of Iowa State University is a friend whose advice and encouragement have been invaluable. Professors Steffen Schmidt, James McCormick and Young Kihl, all of Iowa State, contributed valuable comments at the crucial proposal stage. Professors Samuel Beer of Harvard and Ira Katznelson of Chicago also generously encouraged the project as did Professor Richard Rose of the University of Strathclyde.

I must also acknowledge the support of my family and friends: Ben Halpren and Sharon Ackel; my parents, Margaret and Ralph Dorfman, as well my children, Debbie and Lori, who with good humour suffered my absence at night and at the weekends. And, finally, I owe another enormous debt to my wife Penny for her confidence and tireless help.

October 1978   G.A.D.

1 The Problem of Economic Paralysis in Britain: a brief Introductory Review

This study explores the possibilities that British government will be able to overcome the problem of repeated economic paralysis. It focuses specifically on the relationship between the union movement and the government in the management of the economy since 1968. It takes the view that, in spite of periodic industrial conflicts, government for the first time is gradually winning the cooperation of trade unionism for effective economic management. This change is the result of involuntary developments and not the success of a frontal attack on trade union power. Such attacks as first the Wilson Labour and then the Heath Conservative governments undertook between 1968 and 1974 were spectacular failures which enhanced rather than diminished union power and intransigence. In contrast, Britain's worst post-war recession coupled with the growing internationalization of economic decision-making and especially British entry into the European Communities are combining to endow government with new leverage. The consequence is that trade unionism now has a greater stake in cooperation as well as a greater fear of conflict than at any other time during the post-war era.

I THE HISTORICAL LEGACY: PARALYSIS AND STAGNATION

The significance of Britain's economic problems for its politics is confirmed daily in the British press. British politicians have debated for decades about how government might solve the country's seemingly endless series of economic crises. The problem at its simplest is that Britain suffers from being a very populous nation with a relatively high standard of living which consumes more foreign goods than it can afford. Lack of domestic raw materials, an antiquated industrial base, the rise of more modern, aggressive foreign competitors all contribute to the problem.[1] So too does the relationship between the trade union movement and the British government.

The importance of union-government interaction is illustrated by the comments of many observers that the union movement is to blame for much of Britain's economic difficulties.[2] They charge frequently that the unions have selfishly pressed their narrow sectional demands for higher wages and lax productivity standards to the great harm of the larger national interest.

Such complaints about union responsibility for Britain's economic well-being owe their origin to the period at the end of the Second World War. In 1944 the major political parties agreed that government should undertake to manage the economy in order both to defend against renewed depression as well as to create a high and rising standard of living.[3] The centrepiece of the government's new purpose was to create and maintain full employment.[4] No other deprivation caused by the economic depression during the twenties and thirties so ravaged British morale. Political leaders therefore recognized that full employment was a first priority. The new teachings of Keynes, moreover, seemed to provide the ideal formula by which government could guarantee delivery on this promise.[5]

As a consequence of those new policies, the trade union movement through its spokesman the Trades Union Congress (TUC) was drawn by government from the fringes of power into the centre of national economic decision-making. For trade unionism, the development of full employment provided the linchpin for a vast increase in its power. The new scarcity of labour ensured positive leverage in collective bargaining so that British unionists for the first time in nearly three decades could expect to win progressive wage increases. At the same time this leverage ensured union influence with government, which worried that unrestrained wage increases might endanger the cost-competitiveness of British exports. In sum, government by its management of the economy came to need the advice, acquiesence, and cooperation of trade unionism.[6]

The most cursory review of British economic history since 1945 reveals that government has failed to achieve most of its purposes and has equally failed to enlist trade union cooperation, advice or even acquiesence. The issue of wage restraint has been the most contentious. Conflict raged on many occasions as government repeatedly demanded cooperation on this issue. The decline of the British economy into a series of crises made these demands more urgent and the argument between unions and government more bitter.

Of government's four attempts to attain union cooperation for wage restraint between 1945 and 1968,[7] only one attempt was successful, that of 1948. The other three (in 1956, 1961 and 1964–67) all ended in failure, with government choosing alternative policies which worked very badly, recycling the problems which the government was attempting to solve in the first place.

Trade union opposition to wage restraint or incomes policy was rooted in the fundamental objection that such an approach unfairly interfered with the rights of working people to bargain freely for the terms of their employment. Union leaders quite easily took this view, which coincided with the demands they heard from their local constituencies that trade unionism take advantage of the bargaining leverage which full employment was providing. These same leaders, operating from London where they had close contact with government, also recognized the larger national interest argument. But they acted from the sectional viewpoint except when they were impressed with the force of party ties or by extreme economic circumstances which seemed to impose overriding considerations.

This process can be documented. For example, the TUC decided quickly to defend sectional interests whenever a Conservative government bid for wage cooperation, which happened twice before 1968, in 1956 and again in 1961.[8] The union movement felt a strong class-tinged hostility toward the Conservatives which it could use to advantage when a Conservative government was in office because the Tories themselves feared union power. Prime Ministers Eden, Macmillan and Home followed Churchill's advice to his Minister of Labour, Water Monckton, that he should avoid conflict with the unions at any cost. Their experience in the General Strike of 1926, mingled with a concern about their personal distance from union membership and their ignorance of the union movement, gave them a disadvantage in the collectivist relationship. Therefore Tory governments hesitated to ask the TUC for cooperation in the first place and when they did so reluctantly the TUC could refuse that cooperation without fear of reprisals. In fact, TUC leaders gained prestige with their membership by their intransigence toward Tory governments.

The union relationship with a Labour Government was quite different because it was "family" matter. The Trades Union Congress and the Labour Party comprised the industrial and political sides of the labour movement. Thus it was not surprising that the Attlee Government in 1948 provided the only example of union cooperation for wage restraint in the years before 1968.[9] Senior trade union officials were reluctant to make that agreement but they "gave in" to the familial pressure of their Labour colleagues, who warned not only of possible economic calamity but of the return of the hated Tories to power. In short, the ties of personality, doctrine and common experience as well as sentiment all worked in that moment of post-war economic crisis to produce a cooperation which the Conservatives could not have won in similar circumstances.

Many of these same considerations worked again in 1964 and 1965 when the Wilson Government successfully pressured the TUC General Council to cooperate in another period of wage restraint.[10] But, this time, the TUC leaders operated from a weakening position of authority. Shop stewards and their rank and file were fed up with government demands. Their view was that it progressively made less difference which political party held office. Both interfered with the proper job of union officials, which is to win immediate, substantive gains in material welfare and not to fall into what they saw as a trap posed by the subtler, abstract arguments about the advantages of serving the national interest by postponing present wage increases in order to win "real" gains some time in the future.

This militant argument as it was used by shop stewards in 1967 to sabotage government's hard-won agreement for TUC wage restraint proved to be a watershed. Labour politicians joined with their Conservative colleagues in reaching the conclusion that collectivist politics was a failure, that the union movement's ability to paralyse economic policy was intolerable. The spectacle of the rising number of wildcat or unofficial strikes was the most obvious symptom. Worse though, these political leaders believed that militant unionists were intent on extending their aggression from the economic sector to the political system itself. By early 1968 leaders in both parties were laying plans for a counterattack. They hoped to restore discipline and authority to the trade union movement while reducing its power and influence over the economic decision process.

II THE COUNTERATTACK SINCE 1968: VOLUNTARY FAILURE, INVOLUNTARY SUCCESS

The central purpose of this study is to examine that counterattack over the years since 1968 in order to throw additional light on the prospect that collectivist politics in Britain might work at last to produce economic stability or even prosperity. The success of that effort from its beginning rested on the development of coinciding incentives for unions and government to cooperate; or, at the least, on the development of government leverage which would effect union cooperation or perhaps acquiesence.

(a) VOLUNTARY FAILURE

The counterattack against trade union power beginning in 1968 sought the latter goal by means of a formal change in the rules of the collectivist relationship. The Wilson Government and then the Heath Government in different ways and to a different degree hoped to wrest the advantage from the TUC. The Wilson Government tried to legislate restraints on militant behaviour which would be sufficient to restore the authority of union leaders. The Government expected that these leaders in turn would be susceptible to the same familial pressures for cooperation which George Brown had skilfully used.

The Tory Government led by Edward Heath started from a completely different view. The Tories accepted that they suffered an inherent disadvantage in any collectivist interaction with the TUC. Therefore, the Heath Government sought to develop a framework of law as well as an economic policy which would put that relationship on "automatic pilot". The law, enforced by the courts, would constrain industrial behaviour. Their economic policy simultaneously would operate without need of any active "advice, cooperation or acquiesence" from the TUC.

Both approaches failed miserably between 1968 and 1974. Their common weakness was that they were susceptible to union negative power, albeit veto power, which they were designed to reduce or end. The power flowed from government's commitment to manage the economy to provide economic security and well-being, rather than from the institutional arrangements and rules which the political leadership attacked. Political leaders seem to have understood this problem from the beginning. But they felt constrained from changing the terms of economic commitment because they believed that the political bidding process in Britain continued to demand their fidelity to its terms and especially to full employment. The outcome of the attack and of the ferocious struggles between the unions and government thus clearly reconfirmed union power and even carried it to new heights.

(b) INVOLUNTARY SUCCESS

The first signs of a much more potent challenge appeared while the new Wilson Government was already reconfirming union strength by legislating a series of TUC-sponsored policies. Recession almost perversely came to the rescue of Britain's battered political elite. Very high unemployment together with hyperinflation proved to be a far more effective counterattacking weapon against union power. They worked to undermine orthodox Keynesian views and by 1975 caused the Labour Government quietly to abandon involuntarily many of the 1944 commitments, including full employment. Gradually in the years after 1975 the basis for union strength slipped away as the Labour Government began "reluctantly" to administer a more monetarist approach to economic management.

This development in turn exposed an important TUC weakness which had previously been little noticed: that the TUC's power is limited and overwhelmingly negative. It was certainly true that the TUC wielded enormous negative influence during the era of full employment. But even during those years the TUC had consistently failed to convince government of either party to adopt alternative policies which it favoured. This weakness had not been crucial so long as government faithfully maintained its commitment to the 1944 agreement. It became crucial, however, beginning in 1975 when the Labour Government gradually abandoned these commitments. The TUC found itself at that time with only limited strength to use in responding to its constituents' demands that it convince government to adopt remedial policies for soaring inflation and the rapid decline in the standard of living.

The TUC began during that same year to look beyond its domestic relations for other remedial approaches. It turned especially to Europe, whose influence on British economic decision-making promised to become more important in the wake of the referendum which confirmed British membership in the European

Communities. Moreover, the TUC recognized that the revival of the national economy depended to a great extent on reflation undertaken by the wealthier European nations.

The TUC's General Council thus undertook its first policy initiative in Europe beginning during the fall of 1975. This effort, however, posed new opportunities for British government as well. European or EEC issues might induce the development of coinciding "British" interests which could foster cooperation between Britain's trade union movement and its government. This cooperation in turn might spill over into producing a new collectivist relationship at home. The contrasting possibility is that British government might enjoy new leverage compelling cooperation by offering to promote union interests in Europe in return for a greater measure of "voluntary" cooperation at home.

The British government might now overcome the problem of economic paralysis. Recession, combined with union recognition of new economic and political realities, seem to be producing coinciding incentives for cooperation.

2 Confrontation Politics: the Labour Government's *In Place of Strife*, 1968–69

The long argument between unions and government in Britain about what influence unions should have in national economic policy-making came to a head in 1968. The fundamental question at issue was how power in the modern British political system would be distributed between the traditional Parliamentary system and the emerging functional system of representation.

Industrial relations was the key issue. Political leaders worried that the rising tide of strikes and other forms of industrial disruption posed a threat to their own authority. Leaders from both parties watched in dismay as militant shop stewards wrecked the agreement for wage restraint which George Brown laboriously worked out with TUC leaders. Collectivist politics, which had always worked poorly, now seemed a nearly hopeless approach.

The Wilson Cabinet was particularly disturbed by these events. Militant sabotage of the incomes policy not only hurt its economic management but put the government at considerable political risk. Harold Wilson himself had staked a great deal on being able to work cooperatively with the unions. He had boasted during the 1964 election that a Labour Government under his stewardship would enjoy a special relationship with the unions which would provide the kind of effective government the Tories could never deliver.

Horrified by the growing militant challenge, Wilson in 1968 took up the strategy of counterattack against union intransigence. He and his colleagues decided that their primary goal should be to restore the authority of union leaders. They reasoned that these national leaders had shown themselves susceptible to the force of familial pressure for cooperation which they would be likely to resume if the flow of power toward local unionism could be reversed.

Wilson recognized that he could more effectively counterattack by striking at the basis for union power: at full employment and the other guarantees developed in the 1944 all-party commitment to economic security. But he dismissed this approach immediately because the basis for his government's political support rested firmly on its promise to fulfil and even enhance the terms of that agreement. Therefore, he decided on an industrial relations strategy which he knew from the beginning would raise considerable resistance from his union colleagues. The risk, however, seemed necessary under the circumstances.

Two key documents published in 1968 provided the catalyst for the Wilson Government to take action. The first was the report of the Royal Commission on Trade Unions and Employers' Associations[1] which Wilson himself had appointed three years earlier to study the role of modern trade unionism. The other document was the report of the Conservative examination of the same subject entitled *Fair Deal at Work*.[2] Together they greatly enhanced and sharpened the growing societal debate about how to deal with union intransigence.

These documents appeared at the height of industrial disruption in 1968 but owed their origin to the earlier arguments about the role of trade unionism which had raged during the run-up to the 1964 election. They offered proposals therefore that sharply differed in the same way that the two major parties in 1964 disagreed over the need to take action against the unions. The Conservative Party was then just concluding thirteen years in office during which it had suffered at the hands of union intransigence on a number of occasions.[3] It was painfully aware that the union movement held the advantage in a very intimidating and unrewarding relationship. By contrast, the Labour Party, encouraged by Harold Wilson, was fully confident that it would have much better luck in office. Therefore, Prime Minister Wilson was initially uninterested in trade union reform while his loyal opposition took up the question with considerable relish.

The Prime Minister in fact openly opposed the concept of a Royal Commission. He agreed to the project only at the urging, ironically, of the Trades Union Congress and particularly its General Secretary, George Woodcock.[4] Woodcock expected that the disgruntled Tories would produce an aggressive plan to destory voluntary trade unionism in Britain. He hoped therefore that a Royal Commission sponsored by a friendly Labour Government would take pre-emptive action by producing arguments and recommendations for the strengthening of the voluntary system. He also viewed this inquiry as an excellent incentive for the trade union movement itself to launch an effort to organize more effectively to take advantage of its new-found collective strength.

But the Donovan Commission, as the Royal Commission became known from its chairman's name, proceeded much more slowly than anyone expected. Its final report did offer the sort of recommendations that Woodcock wanted. However, by then the Labour Government was anxious to take remedial action, not defend voluntary trade unionism.

THE ROYAL COMMISSION ON TRADE UNIONS AND EMPLOYERS' ASSOCIATIONS: THE DONOVAN COMMISSION

The key argument in Donovan was written by Hugh Clegg, a Professor who was well known for his voluntarist views. Clegg spoke directly to the problem of conflict and unofficial strikes. He reasoned that "Britain has two systems of industrial relations. The one is the formal system embodied in the official institutions. The other is the informal system created by the actual behaviour of trade unions and employers' associations, of managers, shop stewards and workers."[5] Clegg went on to argue, and the Commission agreed, that

> The formal and informal systems are in conflict. The informal system undermines the regulative effect of industry-wide agreements. The gap between industry-wide agreed rates and actual earnings continues to grow. Procedure agreements fail to cope adequately with disputes arising within factories. Nevertheless, the assumptions of the formal system still exert a powerful influence over men's minds and prevent the informal system from developing into an effective and orderly method of regulation. . . .
>
> Any suggestion that conflict between the two systems can be resolved by forcing the informal system to comply with the assumptions of the formal systems should be set aside. Reality cannot be forced to comply with pretences.[6]

Taking this analysis further, the Commission pointed out that

> The central defect in industrial relations is the disorder in factory and workshop relations and pay structures promoted by the conflict between the formal and informal systems. Effective and orderly collective bargaining is therefore required over such issues as the control of incentive schemes, the regulation of hours actually worked, the use of job evaluation, work practices and the linking of changes in pay to changes in performance, facilities for shop steward and disciplinary rules and appeals. In most industries such matters cannot be dealt with effectively by means of industry-wide agreements. . . . Factory-wide agreements can however provide the remedy.[7]

National unions or the TUC and the employers' associations thus could not be relied upon to take the leadership in this effort at reform. They were too remote and irrelevant to the new patterns of employee-employer relationships that were developing in individual enterprises. Likewise, the growing problem of unofficial strikes could not be solved nationally but again by reform of the local institutions ". . . of whose defects they [unofficial strikes] are a symptom".[8]

The Donovan Report's substantive recommendations for change followed from this analysis, but throughout took care to preserve voluntarism as the basic characteristic of the British system. The major proposal was for the creation of an Industrial Relations Commission which would receive industrial relations cases on reference from the Department of Employment and Productivity. The Commission would be able to deal with a wide variety of problems and disputes but its work would be limited by the power of the Department of Employment and Productivity to decide what it should examine and by the wholly advisory nature of its findings. The Commission in its work would attempt to convince, persuade, clarify, emphasize, and illustrate the public interest, etc., *but would not be able to order, to direct, or otherwise see that its recommendations took effect*. Likewise, the Commission rejected other possible reforms that smacked of compulsion such as strike ballots, legally enforceable contracts with sanctions against those who break contracts (as do those who wage unofficial strikes). "None of these measures [the Commission asserted] promises any success in the sense of improving our industrial relations as long as the underlying causes of the strikes have not been removed."[9] In sum, the Commission accepted the view that

Many of those who conduct industrial relations in Britain are content with things as they are, because the arrangements are comfortable and flexible and provide a very high degree of self-government. Existing arrangements can be condemned only because these important benefits are outweighed by the disadvantages: the tendency of extreme decentralization and self-government to degenerate into indecision and anarchy; the propensity to breed inefficiency; and the reluctance to change.[10]

The remedy for these disadvantages in every instance lay in modifying voluntarism only to the extent that the state should take a persuasive role in encouraging the peaceful and speedy resolution of disputes and of fundamental reform of workplace relationships.

THE TORY VIEW: *FAIR DEAL AT WORK*

One month before Donovan was published the Conservatives hurried their own study and recommendations into print. *Fair Deal at Work*[11] was produced from four years of study and debate within the Conservative Party. It minced no words. It forcefully argued that government has the duty to "step in" to see that "irresponsible elements" did not abuse their rights to the detriment of national interests or the basic rights of all individuals. The Conservatives were confident that a relevant and sensible framework of law, while providing no panaceas, could help to improve stability and cooperation.

Fair Deal at Work focused its recommendations on what its authors believed were the unrestrained and unfair advantages enjoyed by trade unions. The report complained that Britain was the only industrialized nation without a comprehensive legal structure for industrial relations. The few pieces of legislation that had been enacted, the report said, were responses to new situations largely growing out of specific judicial decisions. The sum of this legislation allowed trade unions to operate with unrestrained advantage. Specifically, the Conservatives complained that:

1. Trade unions are immune from litigation for any of their activities which are not a conspiracy to commit an unlawful act or use unlawful means. "Thus no one can sue a union for negligence, deceit, threats of injury, libel, slander, etc. Furthermore, unions are

not liable for the actions of their own officials – even if the Executive has authorized such action."[12]

2. Collective agreements cannot be directly enforced.

3. "No one has a legal right to join a trade union: unions can make whatever rules they like about whom they will accept, or retain, in membership. Yet, at the same time, the law gives legal protection to people who obtain the dismissal from employment of non-members. Thus, in practice, unions can become hiring and firing agencies: . . ."[13]

4. "The Minister of Labour [later of Employment] has power to inquire into the causes of an industrial dispute . . . but can only appoint an arbitrator if *both* parties agree.

"The Minister can also set up a Court of Inquiry, or a Committee of Investigation . . . There is no power, however, to enforce the findings or recommendations of either body – although the Report of any Court of Inquiry must be laid before Parliament. [The Conciliation Act 1896]

"The Industrial Court is a permanent independent Tribunal. It is not a court of law and cannot subpoena witnesses or take evidence on oath. Its decisions are not legally enforceable – though once they have been accepted or acted upon by the parties concerned they may become an implied condition of the contracts of employment effected."[14] [The Industrial Courts Act 1919]

5. "Only by declaring a State of Emergency can the government act to safeguard essential supplies and services, and it cannot order strikers back to work. . . . The Emergency Powers Act cannot be invoked solely on grounds that the national economy is endangered nor on general grounds of social hardship."[15]

These advantages, the report goes on to argue, are economically and socially unjust and "detrimental to responsible union activity. They were introduced in conditions which no longer exist."[16] Unions must take account in their behaviour of the national interest and when their actions ". . . can mean the difference between employment and unemployment, their internal administration cannot be regarded as a private matter".[17]

The report then goes on to make major concrete proposals for change:

1. Trade unions and employers' associations should be redefined in law, registered, and upon registration, be given corporate legal status. Thus trade unions and employers' associations could sue or be sued over any agreements they have made with individuals or

other collective bodies. They would be liable for torts committed by themselves or their leaders except in a lawful trade dispute, and their funds would be at risk.[18]

2. The legal definition of a trade dispute should be changed. "We see no justification for granting special legal protection to combinations of employers or workpeople who induce, or take part in, certain types of disputes which, in modern conditions, we regard as neither necessary to support legitimate claims nor desirable in the national interest."[19] Thus the definition of a "trade dispute" should be amended to exclude the following:

A. " 'Sympathetic' strikes or lockouts and the practice of 'blacking' the goods and services of a different employer who is not in dispute with his employees."[20]

B. Inter-union disputes in which the employer has no interest whatsoever.

C. Strikes or other coercive action that are called to press for "closed" or "union" shops.

D. Strikes or other coercive actions designed to press an employer not to hire employees for certain kinds of work for which they are qualified.

3. Agreements between employers and unions should become legally binding except as the two parties agree otherwise. Collective agreements would thus be on a par with other contracts.[21]

4. A Code of Practice for industrial relations should be legislated that could serve as a guide to good behaviour for both employers and employees. This Code of Practice should not be directly enforceable, but it should be "taken into account" by arbitrators, boards of inquiry, government departments and a new Industrial Court.

5. A National Industrial Court should be established as a branch of the High Court, and there should be regional divisions to sit in the main industrial centres. Such a court system would hear and decide questions of inter-union disputes, questions of interpretation and breaches of contracts, actions against unfair dismissal, etc.

6. The Minister of Labour (Employment) should be empowered to take the initiative in the conciliation of disputes; should be able to refer disputes to the Industrial Court for arbitration where the government believed the national interest was threatened; be able to apply to the Industrial Court for an injunction to stop a strike or lockout for a specified period while negotiations continued; and should be able to order a secret ballot of employees involved in a

dispute. The Minister could, however, only exercise the last three powers after receiving the report of a fact-finding Board of Inquiry.

PRELUDE TO BATTLE

It was Barbara Castle who took on the job of developing the government's response to these conflicting sets of recommendations. Mrs Castle had no experience in industrial relations but she did have the more important credential of optimism that she could accomplish the great political finesse of developing collectivist cooperation between unions and government which had so long eluded every other politician. That optimism had attracted Harold Wilson's attention during a meeting with her in March 1968. Peter Jenkins relates that Mrs Castle literally talked herself into a switch from the Ministry of Transport to the newly created job of Secretary of the Department of Employment and Productivity, successor to the Ministry of Labour.

She had complained to the Prime Minister that day that the government had proceeded in the wrong way in dealing with the unions. It had continuously made demands for crude and negative wage restraint that could only act as a disincentive to cooperation. Any policy, she said, should be " . . . a positive instrument of socialist planning", with the emphasis " . . . on increasing productivity, not on holding back wages".[22] She was confident that given incentive to cooperate trade union leaders would soon rally to the support of their Labour Government.

The first task though was to restore discipline to the trade union movement.[23] She agreed fully with the Prime Minister that the government should take the initiative in reforming industrial relations. The immediate goal would be to restore the power of national union leaders. She believed the task was urgent because the emergence of Hugh Scanlon and Jack Jones as the new leaders of Britain's largest unions was symptomatic of the growing power of militancy spawned at the local level. The real danger was that the conflict between national leaders and local activists would soon be resolved in favour of local militant power. That process must be reversed, she and the Prime Minister agreed.

At the TUC, the General Council and its staff heard disturbing rumours.[24] There was no longer much doubt that the government was preparing to take some kind of initiative. Donovan, the Tory document, public opinion polls, media criticism and the Prime Minister's well-known dismay at union militancy all conspired to make this prediction seem certain. But at Congress House the pessimism also acted to produce a growing determination among both moderate and militant members of the General Council to fight back with every bit of strength.

Whatever their philosophical differences about pressing wage demands, these different factions had no trouble whatsoever in agreeing that a government initiative would constitute an attack against the basis and instrumentality of modern trade union power. Such an attack would thus obviously pose an intolerable threat. They simply could not accept the loss of influence which they believed was absolutely essential to the exercise of their proper function as guardian of working people's interests.

The General Council was disappointed that "their" Labour Government would so expediently and callously join the chorus of Tory critics who were only "too anxious to do something about the unions".[25] It seemed to many of them that Labour politicians had made little effort to understand the dynamics of the militant–moderate argument. Moderates blamed Wilson and his colleagues for producing much of the trouble by constantly making demands for cooperation on the basis of the "national interest", whose terms politicians had defined without the slightest reference to TUC views. This arbitrary behaviour, moderates complained, simply played into the hands of shop stewards and militant leaders at the national level. It bolstered substantially their argument that it mattered little what government was in office, because trade unionism should press the advantages of full employment at all times and using whatever tactics might be necessary. The possibility that the government might attempt now to move against union power only worsened the situation because the challenge closed the ranks between opposing philosophies in favour of a united defence of what union leaders were all agreed were "basic union rights to consultation, access, and influence".[26]

The General Council was equally appalled at the suggestion that the Labour Government would even consider developing reforms which would intrude the law into industrial relations. British unionism for more than a hundred years had struggled against judicial opinion, which had frequently operated to restrict union activities as being in restraint of trade. The very coalescence of the union movement, the founding of the TUC in 1868 and subsequent union political activity culminating in the formation of the Labour Party itself in 1900 owed much to union defence against the judiciary and its application of the law. It seemed almost bizarre to union leaders in 1968 therefore that "their" Labour Government would turn to the law as a means of attacking the power of the industrial wing of their labour movement.

The TUC's Economic Department advised the General Council to move pre-emptively in this situation.[27] It recommended that, as a first order of business, the TUC concentrate on repairing its access and influence with Labour ministers while developing its own plan for voluntary reform. There was a strong feeling at Congress House that whatever Wilson's personal bitterness or the level of political clamour he would never press industrial relations reform so far as to cause a rupture between the two wings of the labour movement.[28] That sort of break would smack of the disastrous split produced by Ramsay MacDonald in 1931. Therefore, the TUC staff reasoned that the Government eventually would be more than happy to use evidence of TUC determination to reform in order to end the controversy over its own plans.

The General Council was acting on this advice when it pressed Mrs Castle for a meeting in early July 1968 to discuss her views on industrial relations. TUC leaders were anxious to make their own case for voluntary reform to her before senior civil servants could convince the new Minister to take the much harder line which they favoured. Mrs Castle certainly held a reputation for having strong views about many issues but the TUC worried that she would be especially susceptible to her staff in this situation because she was inexperienced in industrial relations.

The meeting proved to be a rude shock for the TUC. Mrs Castle made it clear from the beginning of the session that she did indeed already hold strong views.[29] She seemed to have reached full agreement with the Prime Minister about her marching orders and they clearly were to develop proposals that would be far closer to *Fair Deal at Work* than to Donovan voluntarism. Under close questioning, she even hinted that she was thinking of providing for sanctions against "unconstitutional" industrial action.

The General Council after only a few minutes found itself waging a wholesale defence of what they believed were the rights of trade unionism. Several representatives warned Mrs Castle that she must not attempt to prescribe union behaviour. Unions must continue to have the ability to protect their sectional interests. Government should encourage voluntary reform in order to create a more effective union movement, certainly not legislate to create a more pliant one.

Both sides left the meeting depressed. TUC representatives were horrified by what they heard.[30] Mrs Castle seemed fixed already in views that would inevitably lead to serious conflict. She also seemed determined to avoid serious dialogue, as though she hoped to circumvent the problem of "familial" influence that might deter or deflect her from her plans.

Mrs Castle, for her part, was dismayed.[31] TUC leaders seemed as negative and defensive as she had been told to expect. They seemed to her to be simply concerned that government should not intrude into any aspect of their behaviour; she could not accept TUC soothings that they could produce and implement their own reform. There was no question in her mind that unions could become an important contributing partner in the building of a social democracy, but the meeting had reinforced her impression that government would have to take the lead in developing that relationship.

Mrs Castle accordingly pressed her staff to draft a Consultative Document as the first stage in the development of legislation. The DEP sent the document to the TUC for its comments in late July. The TUC then worked for several months on its answers to the 42 questions under seven headings which the Consultative Document raised. George Woodcock throughout this exercise stressed his view that the TUC must answer the document in a way which would legitimate the argument that the TUC should undertake the reform itself.[32]

During this same period, the TUC took the initiative in reaching an agreement with the CBI pledging both organizations to improve voluntary industrial relations. They agreed to strengthen national bargaining as well as negotiating processes in the factories. Also, they agreed to establish a system for notifying the Department of Employment and Productivity (DEP) about collective agreements and industrial relations policies and to cooperate in establishing the Commission on Industrial Relations. The agreement did not mention sanctions or penalties of any kind.

It was not until the Friday before Christmas 1968 that the TUC learned that its arguments had not deterred the government. Barbara Castle that day asked George Woodcock to come to her office.[33] She showed him the full draft of her proposals. As General

Secretary he was clearly the key spokesman at the TUC but Mrs Castle invited Woodcock alone because she wanted his private advice about the possibilities for winning at least union acquiesence for her proposals.

There has been controversy about what advice George Woodcock gave to Mrs Castle after learning about her proposals that day. One version is that Woodcock was quite optimistic, telling the Minister that "I don't think there is anything in this to which the unions can fundamentally object."[34] The alternative version disagrees, contending that Woodcock directly told Mrs Castle that of the 25 recommendations 17 would be acceptable, five were not acceptable in the present form, and three were totally unacceptable.[35] These three were:

A. The Government, in the person of the Secretary of State for Employment and Productivity, could take the initiative to impose settlements in inter-union recognition conflicts after the TUC and new Commission on Industrial Relations had both failed to win voluntary settlements.

B. The Government, again in the person of the Minister, could order a 28-day "conciliation pause" in an unofficial (wildcat) strike. While the conciliation pause was in effect, workers would be required to return to work and employers would be required to respect the *status quo* that existed before the strike.

C. The Minister could order a strike ballot when an official strike was threatened in a situation which the Minister found to be a serious economic threat or a threat to the public interest.

The failure of unions, their members or employers to obey any of these Government orders could put the offenders at risk of fines to be levied by a newly vested Industrial Court. There was no provision for jail terms for offenders, but rather the fines were to be compulsorily collected if they went unpaid.

This proposal proved to be essentially identical to the White Paper, *In Place of Strife*,[36] which the government published on 17 January. Mrs Castle had written the first paragraph herself:

There are necessarily conflicts of interest in industry. The objective of our industrial relations system should be to direct the forces producing conflict towards constructive ends. This can be done by the right kind of action by management, unions and Government itself. This White Paper sets out what needs to be done.[37]

"What needs to be done" was then elaborated in a long discussion which offered a number of specific remedies. The sum of the document, as Mrs Castle explained to George Woodcock, was a coherent philosophy of the relationship that should exist between employers, unions and the government. Government, representing the community at large, has a strong interest in industrial relations and a compelling obligation to take the lead in propagating the reform of these relations so that they will better serve both the unions and employers themselves as well as the entire British community. Her proposals would strengthen the trade union movement, she insisted, and allow it therefore to play a more responsible national role.[38]

She pointed especially to those proposals in *In Place of Strife* which either responded to long-standing trade union grievances or imposed wholly new obligations on management to cooperate in facilitating the development of collective bargaining. The White Paper insists, for example, that employers carry the main responsibility for improving employer–employee relations in factories and plants. Employers need to develop new processes and procedures for dealing with disputes which are now susceptible to unofficial strikes because of the poor attitude and communication of management. The Report specifically argues:

> Indeed, many of the "wildcat" strikes which cause so much concern today are the result of management's mistaken belief that it has the right to impose changes in its workpeople without full and adequate consultation and then invite them to go through "procedure" afterwards for the remedy of any grievances. This is to show a complete misunderstanding of what good procedures should be designed to do, namely, to secure the co-operation of employees through their representatives in the changes that affect their working lives."[39]

The White Paper in this vein proposes that unions be entitled to business information about individual concerns so unions could bargain more effectively. It suggests that new legal protection be provided against unfair dismissals—a long standing union demand. It also suggests that consideration be given to the participation of workers on boards of directors. Most importantly, a new Commission on Industrial Relations is to be established, without compulsory powers as the unions had recommended, but armed with the responsibility for seeking conciliation of disputes by helping both sides of industry:

> The C.I.R. will be concerned with ways of improving and extending procedural agreements, for example how to promote suitable company-wide procedures, how to develop acceptable rules governing disciplinary practices and dismissals, how to encourage effective and fair redundancy procedures, how to bring shop stewards within a proper framework of agreed rules in their firm, and how to ensure that they are provided with the right kind of facilities to do their job.[40]

While it is not clear how Woodcock actually responded to these proposals that day, Mrs Castle did proceed without hesitation to press the wider campaign to win acceptance of *In Place of Strife*. Whether Woodcock encouraged her or not, the Minister's claim that she relied on this advice was none the less a serious mistake. Woodcock was still General Secretary of the TUC but the constellation of power within the trade union movement had been changing, and Woodcock was increasingly a voice alone.[41] More militant colleagues expressed a much more conflictual view of TUC–government relations. Moreover, Woodcock himself over many months and during the years of Donovan had argued publicly against any intrusion by government into industrial relations, and certainly he was well known to be opposed to sanctions. Thus, the weight of reason argues strongly against the likelihood that Mrs Castle decided to press her proposals intact simply because the General Secretary of the TUC "could find nothing in them" to which he thought his union colleagues would object.

Mrs Castle's decision to press forward was more likely based on her own strong conviction that she was operating from political strength. She fully expected opposition both from trade unionists and from some Members of Parliament. But she believed that her proposals would be popular, were philosophically sound, and that she could carry the day with her colleagues.

As for trade unionists, she was also confident that after reasoned discussion she would win over the bulk of General Council votes.[42] The lessons of union–government relations since 1965 had argued persuasively for developing *In Place of Strife*. Barbara Castle also believed, however, that there were other lessons from this period which demonstrated that trade union leaders would be secretly pleased to support such reform. She reasoned that they were just as *unhappy* as the government that the shop stewards had sabotaged the incomes policy agreements which they had made with George Brown. Union leaders had been genuinely reluctant to enter in those agreements, but they were reluctant because they expected just the sort of rebellion as had occurred. On the other hand, she believed that in principle they were in favour of the restraint because they wanted both to help protect their Labour Government and especially because they did accept the argument that the national interest required restraint—even if they could not support that position publicly.

The best contemporary evidence that Mrs Castle found for this optimistic view she took from the example of the fight over the extension of statutory pay restraint during the summer of 1968. George Woodcock had given his personal support for the Government's intentions, even in the face of strong disapproval from below which was registered at the TUC Congress and by the Labour Party Conference.[43] Also, the General Council itself had taken a clearly passive role in the argument,[44] even in the face of severe criticism from the shop steward movement.

Mrs Castle believed that the General Council would again acquiesce. She believed they would recognize pure self-interest. Rising militancy was steadily destroying the authority of national union leaders. Mrs Castle was offering by her proposals to restore that authority and she was also offering to take the criticism for doing a job which she believed these leaders wanted done. She believed therefore that both the government and national union leaders had converging interests in restoring central authority. *In Place of Strife* was obviously bitter medicine for any trade unionist but its purpose, she thought, was well timed for the problems at hand. She therefore expected initial hostility from the General Council followed by more reasonable and quiet acquiesence once these same leaders recognized the advantages they could reap from her work.

The course of the actual struggle over *In Place of Strife* showed Mrs Castle to be wrong. The Government never could invoke the political loyalties that it had used so skilfully time and time again over the previous four years. Mrs Castle's proposals struck too directly at the underpinnings of the union movement's industrial and political power. Instead of winning the support of trade union leaders, she convinced them instead to resolve their argument with shop stewards in favour of conflict, not collaboration.

Even more crucially, Mrs Castle seriously underestimated the extent to which the dispute would spill over into party politics. The TUC leadership stayed remarkably clear of the intra-party fight but it was the Parliamentary Party which forced the Government to negotiate an end to the crisis in June 1969. The family relationship within the labour movement thus did intrude into the *In Place of Strife* controversy. But the relationship intruded in a direction that was opposite to what Mrs Castle had hoped. The majority of Labour MPs finally came to the same conclusion that TUC staff originally calculated Harold Wilson would reach earlier: that rupture in the relationship between the industrial and political wings of the Labour Party was a completely unacceptable price to pay for the adoption of his government's industrial relations policy. Harold Wilson himself, at nearly the last moment, reluctantly accepted that view as well.

THE BATTLE OVER *In Place of Strife*

The Minister's first move after she met with Woodcock was to approach the General Council. Whatever encouragement George Woodcock may or may not have given to Barbara Castle about the substance of her proposals, she did take his advice to consult with the General Council before going to the Cabinet. He had cautioned her that she would greatly increase the difficulty of consultation if the General Council believed such contentious proposals came to them already engraven with Cabinet approval.[45] Peter Jenkins in his book argues that this "TUC first" strategy only exacerbated Mrs Castle's ultimate political problems.[46] The Cabinet, he asserts, did not take kindly to being asked to review proposals which they already were seeing debated in the newspapers. It would appear, however, that it mattered little what strategy Mrs Castle employed—the substance of her proposals were inevitably un-acceptable to unionists.

Members of the General Council's Finance and General Purposes Committee met at the DEP Secretary's office on 30 December. Besides George Woodcock, the group included: Frank Cousins, leader of the Transport and General Workers Union, who had long been the most powerful voice of the left but was then nearing retirement; Sidney Greene, leader of the National Union of

Railwaymen and chairman of the important TUC Economic Committee; Alfred Allen; and John Newton, then Chairman of the Trades Union Congress. This group was philosophically quite diverse. Cousins usually took a militant view while Alf Allen spoke generally for the moderates. Sidney Greene was also a moderate, but enjoyed such enormous affection and respect within the movement that he could speak with broader authority about what the General Council would be likely to accept or not accept in terms of its political relationship with the Government.

The reaction of the Finance and General Purposes Committee was therefore crucially important in shaping trade union responses to the Government's industrial relations policy. Its reaction that afternoon accurately predicted the nature of the argument with the Government over the following five months. To a man, including Woodcock, the Committee sharply opposed the proposals for penal sanctions which Mrs Castle laid before them.[47] They disagreed among themselves only about how to fight the proposals. Frank Cousins called for immediate and total rejection of the entire document. The other members were more conciliatory, arguing that further discussions might convince the Government to drop the panel clauses. But they were all agreed from the very first moment that the penal clauses were totally unacceptable and must be opposed aggressively.

The General Council fully concurred with the Finance and General Purposes Committee's view a week later on 7 January 1969. Frank Cousins made a strong plea again that the Council reject the whole package of proposals, but dropped the idea in the face of overwhelming sentiment favouring further discussions with the Government.[48] The General Council's formal reply to the Employment Secretary was nevertheless harsh and unequivocal. The General Council would continue its discussions because the majority felt that the TUC held a responsibility to talk with the Government as well as to display loyalty to "its" Labour Government. But loyalty did not provide that either side of the labour movement could violate the long-standing informal demarcation line for responsibilities. The General Council once again insisted that *it* take charge of industrial relations reform, warning that the Government could only harm that initiative by persisting in its own proposals:

Affiliated unions, in association with the T.U.C., are embarking on a detailed examination of how such changes can best be made on the basis of voluntary action which is at the same time the foundation of free trade unionism and the essential prerequisite if the men and women who together make up the trade union movement are themselves to accept such changes willingly. This process, however, would be impeded if the Government allowed itself to be misled, against the advice of the Royal Commission, by outside criticism which is at best uninformed and at worst ill-intentioned. Any attempt by Government to impose unreasonable and therefore unworkable constraints on the freedom of working people to pursue their legitimate objectives could only harm the relationship between the trade union movement and the Government and between working people and employers.[49]

Trouble in the Cabinet mirrored the TUC's hostile reaction. The Employment Secretary heard criticism for consulting with the TUC and CBI before meeting with the Cabinet.[50] But several Cabinet ministers were far more critical of the terms of the White Paper itself. Jim Callaghan, Richard Marsh, Minister of Transport, Judith Hart, Postmaster-General, Richard Crossman, Secretary for Social Services, and Fred Lee, Chancellor of the Duchy of Lancaster, formed the main body of critics. All argued in varying degrees that the proposals were unworkable in the British context and tradition of voluntary industrial relations. They were especially worried that the proposals, whether workable or not, were not worth the damage they would do to the labour movement. Barbara Castle met this argument by insisting that whatever the union objections the proposals were widely popular, both with the general population and among rank-and-file unionists. She argued that their support would ultimately propel *In Place of Strife* through Parliament and earn grudging union acquiesence. Certainly, she said, the effort was worth the risk given the almost sure loss that Labour would incur if it failed to do anything about the strife in industrial relations. She added soothingly that she expected to impose the proposed new authority only as a last resort, on a reserve basis, and therefore unions had nothing to fear in the way of a real intrusion into their normal and traditional activities.

The argument in the Cabinet was bitter but Callaghan and the others who agreed with him were distinctly in the minority. The Cabinet finally approved *In Place of Strife* on the evening of 14

January after five long meetings.[51] The decision was taken a little more easily in the end because another inter-union dispute, this time at British Steel, served to remind the Cabinet of the intractability of the problem and its impact on a large number of people not even party to the dispute. The minority opposition nevertheless remained unreconciled and there was considerable bitterness all around. Many who sided with Castle and Wilson in the Cabinet were especially annoyed by Jim Callaghan's position which they criticized as purely opportunist. They charged that Callaghan was taking the union side only because he believed the dispute could be used against Wilson's leadership.[52] The charge had some ring of truth but it was not nearly as convincing as the argument that Callaghan had instinctively opposed the sort of confrontation which he believed would grow inevitably out of the Employment Secretary's proposals. He had long enjoyed constituency support within the union movement and therefore found it easy and natural to take this position.

Minority opposition within the Cabinet was matched by opposition within the Parliamentary Labour Party (PLP).[53] The left Tribune Group and a majority of the trade union-sponsored MPs greeted Mrs Castle's proposals very critically. At first, they emphasized the unworkability of her proposals, especially the penal sanctions. Later, a growing number of MPs stressed the damage that the argument was doing to the viability of the labour movement. In January and February, however, Mrs Castle as well as the Prime Minister found the criticism predictable and surmountable. Public opinion polls seemed to fully support this view.[54]

Given this interpretation, Mrs Castle spent most of her effort responding to trade union criticism.[55] She emphasized repeatedly that her penal sanctions were to be held in reserve, that she wished that the trade union movement would reform itself so that the Government would not need to force them to do it and that any successor Conservative Government would press much harsher proposals. She denied repeatedly that her proposals were designed merely to respond to public demands that the Government do something about the unions. No, she said, the problem was real, the national interest was clear and she wanted to strengthen and not weaken the unions. She insisted that she was pro-union, but that the unions had failed so far to reform themselves and therefore the Government merely proposed to provide assistance and encouragement. Surely, she asserted, a close reading of *In Place of Strife* proved that she had given over most of her efforts to promote measures that would strengthen union participation in collective bargaining.

The General Council proceeded to mount an open campaign against the penal sanctions while it continued to develop its own substantive counter-proposal. The connection between the Labour Government and its union brethren was important at this stage, as it was again later in the climactic stages. Whereas TUC leaders usually met with Conservative Ministers only in formal situations, they easily and more frequently met with Labour Ministers in informal sessions. This manner of contact operated throughout the dispute. Interestingly, the informal sessions did sometimes create serious misunderstanding which added to the formal bitterness in relations. For example, both Barbara Castle and George Woodcock (before he left the TUC to become Chairman of the Commission on Industrial Relations in March 1969) drew misperceptions from these informal sessions. Mrs Castle, for one, mistakenly believed from her meetings with Woodcock that the General Council would be more flexible than it was. She subsequently thought she heard reinforcement for her optimism from several moderate union leaders who later met with her in private.[56] She believed that these leaders would take some leadership role in building support for at least part of her White Paper proposals. That kind of leadership never developed and the General Council continued to behave in a way which constantly surprised Mrs Castle and made her more distrustful of their word. In this same vein, many union leaders came away from meetings with her with the impression that she would in the end withdraw the sanctions as soon as she saw TUC progress on their own reforms. And they, like she, came to distrust her word and the prospect for a peaceful solution.

There were, however, other signals which the Employment Secretary apparently misperceived. Besides public opinion polls which showed support for penal sanctions, the influential London press pleased Mrs Castle by its general applause for her proposals. *The Times*, not generally known for its enthusiasm for the Wilson Government, lent its strong support:

The unions would be fool-headed indeed if they try to work up resistance to the White Paper proposals. The compulsory measures are the least that any Government could put forward in the present climate of public opinion. They are certainly far less than the Conservatives propose. It is unlikely that any of them will be much used and they need never be if the unions put their own house in order. The outcry from some Labour backbenchers is little short of ridiculous.[57]

And the *Financial Times* soothed strategic worries by reporting that "Initial reactions last night to Mrs Castle's White Paper on trade union reform indicated that the Government would face a difficult but not disastrous passage in the Parliamentary Labour Party."[58] The additional warning by the *Financial Times* that the major problem for the White Paper was union opposition was not the kind of storm signal that Wilson and Castle were looking for. Their eyes were on the crucial middle of the electorate to whom their proposals were designed to appeal, and also to the great middle of the Parliamentary Labour Party which loyally trooped into the division lobby and gave the Government its majority week after week. As long as those constituencies were secure, the Government would, they believed, have the muscle to ride out the storm and, better yet, probably negotiate union support.

Both sides thus settled down in late January 1969 for what they expected would be a long fight. Mrs Castle told the members of the General Council that the government would proceed slowly and cautiously toward legislation.[59] The bill would not be introduced until November, and during the interim the DEP would draft a series of papers on the 25 proposals which would provide the basis for discussion with the TUC. These discussions would continue into May and it would only be after they had concluded that the DEP staff would actually begin the job of drafting the legislation.

Events over the following two months, however, sabotaged these leisurely-paced plans. Serious industrial strife coupled with militant individual-union protests against the Government's policy produced an increasingly serious challenge to the Cabinet's authority.

The trouble began at the TUC where the General Council in late January heard demands that it act aggressively, that it call a special Congress to organize the fight against *In Place of Strife*.[60] Though moderates each time defeated these proposals with the argument that the government's timetable would allow for debate at Congress in September, individual unions began to take action on their own. The leadership of the TUC's two largest unions, the Transport Workers (TGWU) and the Engineers (AEW), provided a significant catalyst for the move. The Engineers, for example, called in their 17 sponsored MPs.[61] AEW officials were careful to admit that the MPs held constitutional positions but they did bluntly tell them that they should also be careful to recognize their ties to the union movement as well. Similarly, Jack Jones, who had already been designated to replace the retiring Frank Cousins at the TGWU in late 1969, told his group of MPs that although the White Paper had some good features, they should reject it as a whole because its bad features made the policy completely unacceptable.[62] In response, the MPs voted unanimously to accept Jones' recommendation.

Other unions held similar meetings. Meetings between union officials and their sponsored MPs to discuss public issues is a common occurrence even during the quietest periods. However, the tone of this meeting was quite different. Union executives knew they could not instruct MPs but they clearly wished to let their MPs know that for once they were seeking loyalty to union interests beyond the discipline and priority which they normally expected and wanted MPs to give to the Party. The Party this time should come second in their view.

MPs, for their part, were generally very sympathetic to the union view. Many union-sponsored MPs believed that the Government had gone mad and that their task was to convince it to relent.[63] They were more than willing to join in the effort to encourage such a decision. They learned at these meetings just how determined union leaders were to fight *In Place of Strife*. Many of them became convinced from these sessions that there would be political disaster for the Party if the conflict was not ended. Most important, many of them as early as February decided that they would be prepared to oppose the legislation in the division lobbies even at the risk of losing their seats. Barbara Castle seems not to have fully appreciated that the succession of union-sponsored MP meetings expressed more tellingly than any other evidence that the unions would not in the end budge from their intransigence and that they intended to translate their hostility into political rebellion.

Mrs Castle's poor attention might be explained by the storm of problems the Government faced at that same time. Relations in some key industries were going particularly sour.[64] The trouble at the British Steel Corporation continued, demonstrating again the danger of inter-union disputes and the TUC's inability to solve them. In this case, the dispute was between the Iron and Steel Trades Confederation, which monopolized unionization in the nationalized steel industry, and two white-collar unions, the Association of Scientific, Technical and Managerial Staffs and the

Clerical and Administrative Workers' Union, both of whom wanted
to organize workers who had belonged to company staff unions
before nationalization. The white-collar unions had earlier tried
unsuccessfully to call a protest strike in the steel industry, but when
they failed they threatened instead to call a strike in the motor car
industry, where they had more influence. Barbara Castle tried to
head off this dangerous situation by appointing a Committee of
Inquiry. But the Iron and Steel Confederation refused to accept
that Committee's recommendation, which was in favour of the right
of white-collar unions to organize. Faced with the power of the
manual unions which so dominated the steel industry, bolstered by
the TUC's support, the British Steel Corporation itself decided to
settle the problem by also refusing to recognize the inquiry's
findings.

TUC and government weaknesses in the face of Iron and Steel
Confederation threats together with bold white-collar union threats
to hold up the motor car industry as ransom for its demands once
again illustrated the turmoil that plagued British industrial relations. Then, as if further evidence was needed, another bitter
dispute developed at the Ford Motor Company. In this case, shop
stewards called an unofficial strike in defiance of their leaders'
agreement to a new Ford contract. The AEW, one of the unions
involved, responded by withdrawing the endorsement of the
contract and declaring the strike official. It charged that Ford
officials should have been willing to reopen negotiations despite the
earlier agreement. When Ford went to court and won a temporary
injunction, the unions refused to honour the decision and continued
to strike. In the end, Ford lost its case in the High Court on the
argument that the original contract was not considered by the
parties to it to be a binding legal agreement. The case received
prominent publicity and feelings ran high on both sides. Shop
stewards had clearly won their battle by bullying both the Ford
management and their own official leaders.

The dispute was important because it generated such alienation
between both sides of industry and between the unions and
government. The contract had promised a new formula for
industrial peace in the automobile industry. Ford had offered
higher wages and benefits in return for a no-unofficial-strike pledge.
The unions had accepted the agreement because it offered such
attractive inducements, even though it also provided that the
benefits would be withdrawn if union members broke the no-strike

pledge. Shop stewards, however, ultimately objected to this arrangement because they linked what they described as a "penal" clause in the auto contract to the penal sanctions contained in *In Place of Strife*.

Barbara Castle viewed this dispute and the struggle at British Steel with dismay. She took both episodes as evidence that she must persist in her plans whatever the uproar.[65] Newspaper headlines screamed day after day about these conflicts and public opinion more than ever seemed interested in government action to end this disruption.

The battle lines had thus hardened by the time Parliament first debated *In Place of Strife* in early March. The Prime Minister strongly backed his Employment Secretary.[66] He accepted that his Government must not be seen backing down in the face of union intimidation. Quite the contrary, the recent industrial turmoil had obviously revived public interest in doing something about the union problem and there was accordingly political reward to be harvested in taking action.

The fierce rebellion of more than fifty Labour MPs on the vote approving the White Paper on 3 March added little caution to the Government's resolve. Wilson would not be deterred. He had lived through many rebellions and had seen his policies emerge intact. He found far more to agree with in a *Times* assessment of the situation than in the dark foreboding of his more sceptical ministers. *The Times*, in noting that the rebellion was the biggest in the lifetime of this Government, had commented:

> But who cares? . . . They [the Government and public] have seen too many other backbench rebellions, nearly as big and a good deal more bitter, that have not stopped the Government from getting its legislation on the statute books with all its . . . essentials unimpaired. . . . Disaffected Labour back-benchers could luxuriate in protest in the certain knowledge that the Government was in no danger of defeat. Backbench pressure is usually most effective in the game of political poker that often precedes Government's policy decisions. But once Ministers have firmly decided to act, it has been shown time and again that the bigger the rebellion the safer the Government is.[67]

The rebellion didn't stop there though and Wilson later in March faced another attack, this time in the National Executive Committee and with the support of his Home Secretary, Jim Callaghan. Callaghan didn't take the lead at the 26 March meeting of the NEC but he certainly lent the considerable weight of his position as a senior Cabinet Minister to a resolution by the miners' leader, Joe Gormley, that the NEC ". . . would not support legislation on all the suggestions in the White Paper on industrial relations".[68]

Callaghan's support for the motion, which was approved by an overwhelming majority with Barbara Castle sitting at the very same table, was certainly unprecedented. It was also unprecedented for the NEC formally to oppose the policies of an incumbent Labour Government. The action not only infuriated Barbara Castle, who regarded Callaghan's behaviour as treasonable, but it alarmed the other senior Cabinet Ministers who believed that Callaghan was moving to take personal political advantage of the Government's vulnerability.

Although the Prime Minister was away on a trip to Nigeria, his senior colleagues, excluding Callaghan, began to meet together to map a new strategy.[69] The group included Barbara Castle, Roy Jenkins, Dennis Healey, Michael Stewart, Richard Crossman and Fred Peart. They agreed without dissent that something had to be done to restore the Government's authority, which was not only under fire at the NEC but faced another and far more serious attack by MP backbenchers who were then hotly opposing a bill to reform the House of Lords.

After long discussion, the group agreed that they would urge the Prime Minister on his return to agree to legislate a "short, sharp" bill in this session as an urgent matter. The group concluded that Roy Jenkins was right in his advice that the industrial relations bill be passed rapidly.[70] Quick action, he said, would not only help deal with the compelling economic situation but it would nip opposition from the unions and backbench rebels before it had a chance to coalesce to block legislation and thereby wound the Labour Party seriously.

Earlier, senior ministers had discussed this same approach but Barbara Castle had staunchly resisted any change in her time-table.[71] She worried both that the unions would be infuriated by the change in timing and that a short bill would undercut the basic thrust of her proposals. She had argued the case for *In Place of Strife* as a coherent proposal to strengthen trade unionism. To chop up the bill and bring the penal sanctions forward, she believed, would undermine the whole case she had worked so hard to sell to the unions. But even she, in the face of the recent Ford strike and NEC trouble, had to admit that her chances of ever convincing the unions to support the proposals had grown slim. The danger of Callaghan's intrigues, however, had grown rapidly.

Wilson returned home on 2 April to face the collective will of this "inner Cabinet" and the wider debate about the undisciplined behaviour of his Home Secretary, Jim Callaghan.[72] He decided immediately to accept his colleagues' advice and authorize Mrs Castle to bring in the short bill. The final straw in convincing him was the successful rebellion which backbench Labour MPs staged against the government's House of Lords bill. In the wake of that debacle, the Prime Minister decided that he could ill afford to take the risk that the industrial relations policy would suffer the same fate. The time had come, he believed, to do something to recapture the initiative.

FROM CONFLICT TO CRISIS

TUC leaders learned about the decision from friendly ministers, despite the efforts of Wilson and his colleagues to keep it secret until all of the plans were ready.[73] Days before in late March, the TUC had heard rumours that senior ministers were considering a short bill. They thereupon asked to see the Prime Minister, but the meeting was delayed until 11 April, after he had returned from Nigeria and after he had made his still-unannounced decision to bring in the bill.

The 11 April meeting proved to be very important. It opened the climactic stage of the scenario. The TUC wanted first to confirm that there was to be a short bill and then to criticize the government for breaking trust by changing its plans and timing for legislation. It also wanted to restate to the Prime Minister directly the union movement's determination to see this fight to the end and to encourage him to avoid further damaging conflict by taking the TUC's offer to undertake its own reform. As it turned out, though, the meeting did go beyond hot words and countercharges to uncover at least the glimmerings of a route to the solution of what very rapidly was becoming a crisis.

The key exchange of the meeting came after the barrage of bitter words.[74] Wilson had refused to admit that he had decided on the change in timing and then heard TUC charges of bad faith when he said that the government did not feel it ever had a commitment on this subject with the TUC. He had also told union leaders that the government was not going to withdraw from taking an initiative on industrial relations simply because they objected to it. Then, in frustration, Victor Feather, who had just become Acting General Secretary, asked the Prime Minister what the TUC could do or even propose that would impress his government? Wilson's answer proved to be crucially important, though it didn't solve anything at the time: "If the TUC wanted the Government to withdraw its proposals they would have to produce an alternative plan which was equally urgent and equally effective as the Government's would be."[75]

Feather immediately picked up on the Prime Minister's words, repeating them back to Wilson for emphasis. Little came from this exchange at that moment but Wilson seems to have realized that his words carried significance for the negotiations. He repeated the same phrase at nearly every one of the dozens of informal and formal sessions during the next nine weeks.[76] Though his words did not fit the TUC's prescription for voluntary reform precisely, the Prime Minister was indicating that a solution was possible in that direction. It also seemed to the members of the Finance and General Purposes Committee, who represented the TUC in most of the negotiations, that the Prime Minister recognized that a solution would need to avoid a break in relations, a calculation which the TUC had assumed from the beginning.[77] Some of the participants that day describe the mood as like what they imagined the mood to have been in the talks between Prime Minister MacDonald and union leaders in 1931. They felt that this atmosphere for the first time convinced Prime Minister Wilson that a solution had to be found which avoided another rupture. Thus, the meeting was important because both sides seemed to realize and implicitly agree that they had a common stake in reaching a peaceful settlement.

The 11 April meeting did not, however, produce a solution nor was peace just around the corner. Quite to the contrary, the two sides also recognized that each was prepared to do considerable battle over the issues in dispute. The atmosphere was to become even more charged. Within a few days, the Government announced its plans to legislate the short bill as quickly as possible.

The Chancellor, Roy Jenkins, made the announcement in his budget speech on 15 April. He left the details of the bill to Barbara Castle.[78] The proposal for compulsory strike ballots was dropped but the other two proposals for penal sanctions were to be included in this bill. The bill was to provide that when the TUC could not resolve inter-union disputes the Employment Secretary would, under threat of fines, enforce a solution recommended to her by the new Commission on Industrial Relations. Also, the Employment Secretary was to be able to order, again under threat of fines, a 28-day conciliation pause to stop unconstitutional strikes. During this pause, the Employment Secretary could order that the pre-strike *status quo* remain in effect while negotiations continued. The proposed legislation was also to contain other balancing provisions that were generally pro-union and "sweeteners" against the bitter medicine of the penal sections. For example, all workers would have a legal and enforceable right to recognition where there was no inter-union dispute; and, importantly, workers laid off because of a strike in which they were not involved would be able to collect unemployment benefits.

The "sweetening" provisions predictably went almost unnoticed by the unions and the news media, which were busy warming to the growing conflict. Victor Feather commented that the details of the short bill showed that "there has not been much change in the attitude of the Government and certainly there has been no change in the attitude of the TUC general purposes committee".[79]

Separate meetings on 15 April, first with the Employment Secretary to learn the details of the short bill and then with the Prime Minister, provided little new information for the General Council or any movement to solve the impasse. The short bill changed the situation, however, in that it brought the long simmering argument to a head. From 15 April until 18 June the TUC and the Government waged the most intense negotiations that any government ever had with a producing group since government first took up peacetime management of the economy in 1945.

The method for solution to the conflict was at all times before the negotiators. The Prime Minister repeated again on the day Jenkins announced the short bill that if the TUC could produce alternative proposals which would be as urgent, effective, and quick-acting as the Government's he was prepared to "reconsider" the Government's position.[80] The TUC had earlier somewhat timidly taken up that approach in its "Action on Donovan" initiative. "Action on Donovan" promised study and not specific action, especially failing to offer any concrete trade union proposals to deal with the major problem of strikes which most worried the

Government. While the TUC at that 15 April meeting angrily denounced the Government's deceit in changing the legislative timetable and repeated objections to penal sanctions, the full efforts of the TUC staff at Congress House were thrown into the job of taking up Wilson's offer.

Len Murray, then head of the TUC Economic Department, took the major responsibility for drafting the TUC proposals which came to be entitled *Programme for Action*.[81] Trouble in the Parliamentary Labour Party, on the National Executive Committee and in the Cabinet itself was already quite obvious, so that Murray knew that one goal of his work was to make the TUC document appealing to Wilson as an instrument for getting off the hook.[82] He knew that Wilson and Castle were still committed to their proposals and believed that in an all-out fight they could carry the day. But the pressure for settlement with the TUC was already sufficiently intense to make a settlement based on the Prime Minister's already stated prescription quite attractive.

At the same time, Murray agreed with Feather and Woodcock before him that Government pressure for the TUC to take new powers was a positive opportunity. The indiscipline that unofficial strikes demonstrated within so many unions was obviously also eroding the power of the TUC. While the TUC General Council and its individual union executives were strongly against government's intrusion into industrial relations, they were eager to restore their sagging authority. The problem was how to capture this benefit from the policy without taking the whole policy itself. The possibility that the TUC might run the policy instead was therefore quite attractive.

While the TUC staff was hard at work producing proposals that it hoped would take up Wilson's offer, Feather met with Wilson and Castle for several informal chats and dinner meetings between 16 April and 12 May. Feather worked hard during these sessions to convince Wilson that the TUC's forthcoming proposals would offer the only real basis for compromise.[83] Feather wanted to impress on the Prime Minister the notion that the Government's proposals would not strengthen union leadership in its relations with shop stewards, but instead would give more strength to the militant position that unrelenting conflict would be more beneficial for union interests than any degree of cooperation. He also told the Prime Minister that the TUC had so far provided the Government with a kind of tacit cooperation in that it had stayed out of the political argument which was obviously raging within the Labour Party. However, the TUC could not continue to ignore this powerful leverage if the Government insisted on its penal sanctions.

The General Council debated and approved *Programme for Action* on 12 May, and made plans to present the document to a special TUC Congress already set for 5 June. That afternoon the General Council trooped back to Number 10 to offer their proposals to the Prime Minister and his Employment Secretary. With the question of strike ballots already eliminated from the negotiations, the two remaining contentious issues were inter-union disputes and unofficial strikes. *Programme for Action* proposed strong TUC measures to deal with inter-union disputes and the Prime Minister and Mrs Castle were pleased. The proposal gave the TUC new powers to "intervene in any dispute arising from demarcation or other inter-union problems. The general council would be able to make binding awards. If an individual union refused to accept an award, the general council would be free to suspend it from membership or to report it to Congress with a view to disaffiliation."[84] That sort of "obligation on the unions" was exactly what the Government was looking for. Wilson applauded the proposal as a "viable and equally effective alternative to the Government's proposals".[85]

The strong TUC initiative on inter-union disputes served as contrast, however, for the Prime Minister's unfavourable reaction to the proposals for dealing with unofficial strikes. In a memorable comment, Wilson said that "there appeared to be a missing link between, on the one hand, what the General Council had clearly spelled out they would do in relation to interunion disputes and, on the other, their proposals for intervention in unconstitutional stoppages".[86] Mrs Castle complained that the unions had not indicated what they would do to "ensure that their members returned to and remained at work during negotiations. Without a clearer definition of what influence the General Council would use, the proposal could at best be regarded as a pious hope."[87]

The General Council members in turn replied that the Prime Minister was underestimating the importance that unions would attach to recommendations of a TUC disputes committee. Moreover, if that advice was ignored the General Council could report the offending union to Congress, which could take action to disaffiliate that union. However, there could be no question of applying automatic procedures in the way that the Employment

Secretary seemed to have in mind. Flexibility must apply because each case is different. Moreover, if unions would ever apply direct sanctions against offending local union organizations in an unoffical dispute, national unions rather than the TUC must apply those penalties. The General Council reported that they had examined the rule books of 130 of its member unions and found that all but six had "the power to impose penalties in the form of fines and expulsion for action in breach of rules".[88]

The meeting of 12 May thus ended in continued disagreement but with one of the two issues out of the way. The Government had clearly signalled its satisfaction with the proposal on inter-union disputes and took that proposal as a cue for suggesting that the TUC apply similar obligations and action against unofficial strikes. Three days later, on 15 May, the General Council at its own meeting tried to go a little further but without producing any substantial changes in TUC power. In its first draft of *Programme for Action*, the TUC had proposed to include unconstitutional strikes within the provisions of its Rule 11 which until then provided the TUC with authority to intervene in disputes that threatened the jobs of workers whose unions were not directly involved in a particular dispute. *Programme for Action* suggested that the TUC now be empowered to investigate unofficial strikes as well and make recommendations. At its 15 May meeting, the General Council added new language that emphasized that unions would be required to do all "they could reasonably be expected to do to secure compliance with a recommendation (or an award, where this has been made) including action within their own rules if necessary".[89] The General Council added that "in the unlikely event" of a union refusing to act on a decision of the TUC, the General Council could take action under Rule 13, which included the power to expel offending unions from the TUC.[90]

The General Council then placed a price on *Programme for Action*. The price for making these changes was the Government's agreement to drop the penal sanctions.[91] Unless it did, the TUC would take no action of its own. It was this price, more than anything, that nettled the Prime Minister when the General Council again met with Wilson and Castle on 21 May.[92] Wilson caustically told the General Council that their price for action cast doubt on the seriousness of their commitment for reform. In fact, the General Council's threat reawakened both leaders' deep suspicion about the TUC's power or willingness to do anything on its own.

The question of trust by then dominated the discussion far more than the substance of the disagreement. The TUC believed it had made its concession to solve the dilemma.[93] Members of the General Council therefore took seriously Wilson's public comments that the TUC had moved faster in a short time than it had in the last four decades. And they expected the Government to find some way to accept their terms, even if the Cabinet had to go through the motions of appeasing political demands that it appear tough and resolute. They viewed the impending Special Congress on 5 June as the ideal mechanism through which the Government could find its "out" by the overwhelming support Congress would give for the TUC proposals. The warning to the Government that they would not take voluntary action unless the Government dropped the penal sanctions was a nudge to convince Wilson to grasp the solution which the TUC felt it was handing him.

The hostile tone at the 21 May meeting therefore took many TUC leaders by surprise. They underestimated the extent to which Wilson mistrusted them, and especially how much he mistrusted Jack Jones and Hugh Scanlon. Wilson and Castle had taken the TUC threat to shelve its own plans if the Government didn't drop the penal clauses simply as further evidence that the Government probably could never trust a deal with the unions. Their memory of the sabotaged incomes policy agreement, of contemporary industrial strife, just when Jones and Scanlon came to leadership, was simply too much. Wilson had had his first chance to "do the deal" on that day and he backed away.

Victor Feather, the tireless negotiator and consensualist, was one of the few at that meeting who understood what was troubling the Prime Minister.[94] The Prime Minister wanted automatic protection in any agreement plus some evidence that Jones and Scanlon would not be free to "sabotage" a new relationship. He thought that the General Council could go further and develop the necessary assurances. Feather, however, believed the Prime Minister was misjudging the situation. He felt that Wilson overestimated the lengths to which the General Council could go in doing what the Government otherwise planned to legislate. And he also believed that Wilson underestimated the extent to which the majority of the General Council had come to agree with Scanlon and Jones about resisting the Government's plans. In short, Feather wanted to convince Wilson that the General Council had gone as far as it could or would, that it would help to convince public opinion that its proposals were viable and therefore that Wilson should take the deal. It was with this purpose that Feather organized a meeting between Castle, Wilson, himself, Jones and Scanlon on the weekend of 1 June at Chequers. There are several spicy but accurate accounts of this meeting.[95] One version written by Feather's biographer, Eric Silver, reports that:

> The nearest to acrimony was a private conversation between Wilson and Scanlon, when the engineers' president reminded the Prime Minister of Stalin's famous question: "How many divisions has the Pope?" The repartee soon advanced from Joseph Vissarionovich. Scanlon told Wilson the Labour movement did not want another Ramsay MacDonald. Wilson replied that he had no intention of being another MacDonald. Nor did he intend to be another Dubcek. "Get your tanks off my lawn, Hughie."[96]

While this passage colourfully described some of the atmosphere of that meeting, the substance of the meeting was just as tough. Jones and Scanlon held their ground; they would go no further in compromising elementary trade union rights. Scanlon told Wilson that if the Government pressed its policy of penal sanctions the Prime Minister would be faced with demonstrations and very probably more strikes. The tough talk got Feather's point about the solidity of the union position across but it didn't convince Wilson that he should take the deal. Rather, the meeting steeled Wilson's resolve to hold out against the deal at the moment.[97] He recoiled at what he felt was a union power play designed to take advantage of the obviously difficult situation in the Cabinet and Parliamentary Labour Party. He was appalled at the rude and brash conduct Scanlon and Jones displayed.

Evidence of how the two Government leaders reacted to their weekend at Chequers came within a few days when Castle sent Feather a three-page letter.[98] The letter, which arrived only a couple of days before the Special Congress, raised a number of new objections to the revised *Programme for Action* and restated the other Government criticisms. The letter could have easily destroyed the possibility of Congress support for the TUC's recommendation had it been introduced either to the General Council or the Special Congress. But Victor Feather kept its contents to himself, only informing the General Council that he had received a new letter which he would send round to each of them for their comments. Thus, the Congress on 5 June dealt only with the proposals before them and delivered the sort of overwhelming support for the General Council position that Feather had hoped to win.

The majorities on all three resolutions were about 8 to 1.[99] The large and influential unions stood solidly with the majority. There was a strong feeling running through the hall that day in Croydon that the Government couldn't hold out much longer against the force of this TUC statement. The delegates had overwhelmingly shouted their opposition to fines on unions or working people. They had said "yes" to the other proposals in the White Paper and had given the General Council full authority to go ahead with *Programme for Action*. But the Congress had also served notice that *Programme for Action* must be the limit of compromise. The General Council was not to go any further.

This mood of strength and unity none the less failed to impress the Prime Minister. He had already discounted the Congress in advance and found his experience with Scanlon and Jones more compelling. He continued to insist that any deal must go beyond *Programme for Action*.[100] For her part, Mrs Castle continued to stress that nothing short of legislation would be effective. Both of these sentiments were echoed in the Government's official press statement in reaction to the Congress.[101] The statement acknowledged that Congress had approved a major increase in TUC power but it also re-emphasized that the Government had considerable doubts about the TUC's proposals to deal with unconstitutional strikes. The TUC's plans still suffered from a lack of precision and of assurances that TUC recommendations to solve disputes would be accepted by individual unions and their members.

The General Council next met with the Prime Minister and his Employment Secretary on 9 June. By then, the unfavourable Government press statement coupled with Wilson's own intransigent comments in speeches on tour in the North-East of England had foreshadowed further stalemate. Feather and most of his senior colleagues were discouraged because it seemed that Wilson was determined to push the situation to the breaking-point in order finally to rationalize the need for legislation.[102] The letter from the DEP which Feather had stifled was designed clearly to sabotage the Congress, and his post-Congress statements seemed bent in the same direction. Wilson must now realize, Feather reasoned, that Congress had authorized both the TUC reform and the limits of compromise.[103] The Chequers talks at the very least must also have demonstrated that even Scanlon and Jones felt

constrained by their own executive committees from leading much
further, even if they wanted to do so.

Nothing happened at the 9 June meeting to relieve the gloom.
Members of the General Council again told the Prime Minister that
the TUC could make no new concessions and the Prime Minister
told them that their statement on unofficial strikes had to be
strengthened.[104] He added that the Cabinet would be exploring the
possibility of other forms of sanctions and that it might be possible to
devise different approaches including, for example, giving legislative backing to the TUC's plans or perhaps finding some other
instrument in the Donovan Report. Nevertheless, he said the
government needed to act very soon to deal with the problem of
unofficial strikes which were continuing to besiege the economy. In
the end, both sides agreed to meet on 11 and 12 June, after which he
promised that the Cabinet would decide whether to bring in the
short bill during that Parliamentary session.

The next morning Feather, Wilson and Castle resumed the
private conversations which they had held several times over the
previous few weeks.[105] The Prime Minister sharpened the focus of
his argument. He suggested to Feather that the TUC change Rule
11, which dealt with industrial disputes. Feather immediately
replied that there could be no consideration of a change in the rule,
but the General Council could send a note of clarification to
individual unions explaining how the TUC would operate Rule 11
to deal with unofficial strikes, and that that explanation could have
the precision which the Government wanted.

Feather suddenly thought he saw an opening toward settlement.
But would Wilson and Castle take it? The answer came at the next
formal session the following day, and it was "apparently" no, at
least not yet.[106] Wilson never even mentioned Feather's suggestion.
Instead, the Prime Minister stuck to his demand for a change in
Rule 11 or some other similar alternative including bringing in the
short bill and legislating penal clauses which would be held in
reserve until the TUC could prove that its own plans would work.

General Council members would have none of that.[107] They were
not going to operate the Government's policies or accept what they
strongly believed were unworkable and unfair sanctions of any kind,
reserve or not. More succinctly than before, several members of the
General Council told the Prime Minister that his proposal to
strengthen Rule 11 to match the TUC's stronger plan to deal with

inter-union disputes was simply wrongheaded. Unofficial strikes were quite a different problem from inter-union disputes because they had an "employer element". Grievances often had to be settled *before* workers could return to their jobs. It was sheer fantasy, they said, to think that the unions or the government could always "obtain a resumption of work merely by ordering workers to return to work".[108]

The gloom remained unrelieved that morning, though the talks did not break down. Instead the Prime Minister asked the General Council to appoint a smaller negotiating team of six to carry on even more intensively. There seemed no opening for settlement at that moment, but it was clear to all that the force of the special relationship between the two wings of the labour movement compelled a greater effort.

The new negotiating sub-committee met for the first time that afternoon. It decided to take up Feather's suggestion, already put privately to Wilson and Castle, that the General Council circularize the unions with an explanation of how it would operate Rule 11. The committee proceeded to draft the proposed clarification and later that same day to offer it to the Prime Minister. But though Wilson did find the wording encouraging, he wondered why it could not simply be written into Rule 11.[109]

Another meeting of the sub-committee itself and another meeting of the sub-committee with Wilson and Castle followed that same day. But there was no movement by either side.[110] The sub-committee, consisting of the TUC's most senior leaders, Alfred Allen, Sidney Greene, Jack Jones, Hugh Scanlon and Sir Frederick Hayday (in place of the absent TUC Chairman, John Newton), unanimously rejected some new wording which the Prime Minister had suggested. The Prime Minister and Mrs Castle, in turn, found the TUC circular insufficient. In sum, 11 June was a day of the most intense argument but no agreement. More meetings were set for the next day.

The General Council caucused the next evening at 10 Downing Street immediately before it resumed meeting with the Prime Minister and Employment Secretary. There was quick agreement again that the Prime Minister's wording for changing Rule 11 was totally unacceptable and that the sub-committee had taken the proper approach in suggesting that a note of clarification to Rule 11 be the basis for a final compromise. The full session with Government leaders proved totally fruitless. The Prime Minister told the union leaders that the Cabinet was willing to drop the penal clauses in exchange for a rule change.

> If the General Council would legislate, then the Government would agree not to legislate. The Government's amendments to Rule 11 were small but important and there was not a word included which was not in *Programme for Action*. If the General Council were not prepared to give the assurance for which they were asked, the matter could not be pressed further and at the next meeting on June 18 the Prime Minister would discuss with the General Council the alternative forms of legislation.[111]

The General Council refused to budge. They warned that:

> The General Council's authority in the future, which was now accepted by unions, would be severely prejudiced if they went to Congress with the kind of amendment suggested by the Prime Minister. The TUC would operate on the basis of *Programme for Action* as a whole. No matter what was in the rules the General Council could not guarantee to do more than try to resolve disputes. They could not be 100 per cent effective; nor could any law.[112]

Two days of intense negotiations had produced no change, nor had there been significant movement since the 5 June Special Congress. The TUC's only concession to the Government's stubbornness was its proposal to send a notice of clarification to its unions about how it would operate Rule 11. If the Government wanted help in explaining an agreement on this basis, the TUC made it clear that it stood ready to help. But it would go no further, and Feather had told Wilson and Castle repeatedly that they should not entertain illusions on this score. And yet they scoffed at taking less than a change in Rule 11 in return for dropping the penal sanctions. Both sides thus simply went on repeating their positions to the utter boredom of the other, though at all times careful to avoid pressing the conflict to open rupture.

For their part, the Prime Minister and Mrs Castle struggled with a dilemma. They had staked so much of their own reputation on industrial relations reform, which continuing industrial strife showed was a smart political calculation. Moreover, Wilson's experiences on his recent trip to the North-East had also confirmed his long-standing view that the rank and file and their family supported the Government's initiatives. But the rebellion from within the party coupled with TUC obstinacy in the fight made his policies increasingly vulnerable to defeat. Roy Jenkins, it now seemed, had been right in his advice that June would be too late for legislation.

Wilson had wavered in the face of these considerations after the 5 June Special Congress. For more than a week and a half he held firm against the temptation to take the TUC deal. Barbara Castle certainly proved a strong lobby in favour of toughing it out.[113] The Chequers talk and his trip both made him suspicious that he would rue the day that he made another deal with the TUC. Then there was the steady stream of politicians and even some union officials who informally and in private promised their loyalty and support in the fight.[114] And there were the taunts from the Conservatives who stood only too ready to pick up the political advantage they saw from a government move to back down on its pledge to do something about the industrial relations problem.

The climax was reached on 17 and 18 June. The politics of the labour movement came to dominate all other considerations. Wilson at the last moment refused to trade his career and the future of the Labour Party off for a legislative victory in the House of Commons produced with Tory votes.

A SOLEMN AND BINDING UNDERTAKING

The last chapter in the battle was led as much by backbench Labour MPs as by the TUC General Council. The failure of the 11–12 June talks greatly alarmed the PLP.[115] Victor Feather's gloomy comments that he had been more optimistic a week earlier gave substance to rumours that Wilson was simply playing out the talks as a rationale for pressing legislation. The Cabinet would soon have to take a final decision on legislation and in the absence of agreement it seemed to many that Wilson was about to make the fatal error of pressing a split in the movement.

Douglas Houghton, chairman of the PLP, took the lead for his colleagues in expressing these fears to the Prime Minister.[116] Houghton also took the initiative in developing a continuous communication with Victor Feather, who had become interested in coordinating an effort to place increasing pressure on Wilson to settle.

On Monday 16 June the Liaison Committee added its own pressure, sending Wilson a formal letter warning him against pressing a split in the movement.[117] Wilson never mentioned that letter when he met the Cabinet next day.

He didn't need to. Most of the Cabinet already knew the letter's contents and were themselves near rebellion. They would not give the Prime Minister their support for telling the TUC that either the unions must legislate or the Government would. The Cabinet wanted a settlement; the future unity of the labour movement was far more important to them than the penal clauses. The time had come to settle the argument and Wilson should make the best deal he could when he met the TUC the following morning.

Wilson would have none of this. Time and time again that day he and Barbara Castle tried to rally support within the Cabinet. But in the end, there was no agreement. The Cabinet meeting of 17 June finally came to end after 7 p.m. without an understanding. The Prime Minister would still be in command when he met the TUC the next day, but it was now clear that the outcome of the negotiation would decide much more than the future of industrial relations policy. Wilson's own leadership was at stake, and he knew it.[118]

In his recollections, Wilson discounts the importance of the 17 June meetings in shaping the course of the 18 June negotiations with the TUC. Wilson contends that: "They could not know the line-up, as I did."[119] However, the recollections of so many of the other participants tell a different story. Much as he wrote later, Wilson spent the evening of 17 June fruitlessly trying to convince, first, the trade union group of MPs and then Victor Feather himself that he, Wilson, had the votes to win his policy. But the Cabinet's dissent was well known to Feather and others in the trade union leadership.[120]

When the General Council met with the Prime Minister and Barbara Castle on the 18th, Victor Feather wondered whether Wilson would "go for broke". He knew from Douglas Houghton that the Cabinet meeting had broken up the night before in stalemate. The Prime Minister had held firmly to his position, giving no indication that he was ready to accept his colleagues' advice that he settle.[121] Would he risk his leadership in order to force an agreement from the TUC? If he did, Feather and his colleagues were prepared to resist. They were sure now that the Party would never permit Wilson to carry out his threats.[122] The penal sections of *In Place of Strife* were already dead; the real question now was whether Wilson would insist on his own political destruction. Those among the General Council who knew Wilson best were sure that the Prime Minister would choose to settle.

The 18 June meetings went almost exactly as these union leaders guessed. Wilson pressed them one last time at the beginning. At the outset he warned, as if his political difficulties didn't exist, that if the TUC continued to refuse changing Rule 11 as suggested the situation "was very serious".[123] "If the General Council could not agree to change the form of Rule 11 in any way the Government would have to consider what form their legislation should take . . ."[124] In fact, he went on, the Government had alternatives and he was prepared to meet the TUC objections to "automatic" sanctions. His proposed amendments to Rule 11 could allow that there would be situations when the "General Council would wish to proceed in a different manner".[125]

The General Council briefly withdrew to consider the Prime Minister's statement. After a short discussion the Council instructed its sub-committee to tell the Prime Minister that though they did not quarrel with his new suggestion, there still could be no question of changing Rule 11. The sub-committee carried out this instruction when it resumed talks with the Prime Minister and Mrs Castle.[126] Hugh Scanlon added impassionedly that he had already pressed his own executive committee just as far as he could when he won their support for the actions taken at the Special Congress.[127] To ask them to go further now would be to court disaster. He had won the earlier battle by a handful of votes. If he had to call them into session again to consider any further rule changes he was positive that he would lose that vote and worse, the remaining support for *Programme for Action* would collapse. The defection of his union, the second largest in Britain, would almost certainly reverberate to destroy the work of the last six months.

Fred Hayday of the General and Municipal Workers' Union and Jack Jones intervened in the discussion at this point to make what turned out to be the pivotal suggestion.[128] Hayday suggested that the General Council adopt the Government's wording for the clarification that the TUC had been promising for its newly-approved Rule 11. The General Council could guarantee the clarification as a "solemn and binding" undertaking. Jones added that this kind of binding agreement would have the force of a rule of Congress much as had the Bridlington Principles that Congress had adopted in 1939 and which had effectively provided the rules by which unions competed between themselves for members.

Wilson didn't immediately agree to the proposal but he did seem "relieved". He did go so far as to promise that if there was a settlement on this basis that he would not " . . . propose to proceed with interim legislation on industrial relations; and that they would not include the so-called penal sanctions in the legislation to be introduced next session or in any legislation introduced during the lifetime of the present Parliament, with the proviso that this must be subject to review if the Congress in September failed satisfactorily to endorse the General Council's undertaking."[129]

The TUC sub-committee then reported back to the full General Council while the Prime Minister and his Employment Minister met with their advisers to consider whether to accept the "solemn and binding" agreement. The decision seems to have been taken quickly and during the lunch break the Attorney-General was brought over to draft the statement. Feather then met privately for the last time with Wilson and Castle. While there was some haggling over wording and over whether the General Council members would all sign the agreement – Feather insisted that only he and the TUC Chairman would sign, and he won the point – the disputes were minor.[130]

The agreement was taken to the Cabinet in the late afternoon. It was approved to loud applause. Wilson and Castle then returned to the General Council and the Prime Minister announced the Cabinet's endorsement: "He expressed the hope that the outcome of the discussions would be regarded as a victory for good industrial relations, a view which was fully endorsed by the General Council."[131]

CONCLUDING COMMENTS

Political analysts at the time were less kind in their assessment of the settlement. It had nothing to do with good industrial relations, they argued. It had much more to do with saving Harold Wilson, saving the Government, and saving the Labour Party.[132] What had started out as an effort to produce public policy ended as a narrow argument between the two wings of the Labour Party about demarcation. The interests and the wishes of the public at large had been ignored in finding a settlement.

This criticism was in large measure properly on the mark, Harold Wilson's own heroic account notwithstanding. That the negotiations were in the manner of a rescue operation for the labour movement testified to his failure. He and Mrs Castle started out to re-establish the power of national union leaders so that his Government could once again enjoy the advantages of familial influence for collectivist cooperation. Their strategy did bolster the authority of TUC leaders but not in the way they planned. *In Place of Strife* caused militant and moderate TUC leaders and the shop stewards movement to lay aside their differences for the moment in order to unite in the fight back against Government "intrusion" into industrial relations. The strength of their resistance coupled with the political help of the Parliamentary Labour Party turned the power of familial influence to work in the opposite direction – against the political leadership.

Wilson and Castle in the end not only saw their strategy in ruins but suffered the strengthening of the demarcation between the industrial and political sides of the labour movement in a way which probably forestalled similar "counter-attacks" on union power in the future. Thus, even while the labour movement savoured its self-rescue during the summer of 1969, its political leadership sank into a gloomy mood. Collectivist paralysis now seemed intractable short of Labour's renunciation of full employment and the other elements of the 1944 agreement – a change which was unimaginable at that time. Wilson's boast that he could develop and use effective relations with the unions now seemed like the worst kind of joke and the public opinion polls during that summer predicted that the electorate would register their disgust at the next opportunity.

3 Confrontation Politics: Industrial Relations and Wage Conflict during the Heath Years, 1970–74

Mrs Castle often warned union leaders that the Conservatives would win the next election and proceed to impose their own less merciful formula for industrial relations if she lost the battle of *In Place of Strife*. Mrs Castle proved to be quite right. One year to the day after Wilson and Feather publicly celebrated their "solemn and binding understanding", Edward Heath moved into Number 10 Downing Street fully prepared to "do something about the unions".

Fair Deal at Work stood ready as the guide to Conservative plans to reform industrial relations,[1] and Heath himself had promised the electorate that he would move rapidly to legislate its terms.[2] The Conservative Party solidly insisted that the time had come for Conservatives to take the lead in ending what it saw as the tyranny of unions over economic policy and the nation's industrial productivity. Unofficial strikes, many argued, were only one symptom of the enormous damage that collectivist power had dealt to Britain during the previous twenty-five years.

The Conservative indictment of trade unionism was thus sharper and more comprehensive than Labour's. Labour had also complained about paralysing union power but its remedial proposals focused narrowly on the growing indiscipline of shop stewards who undermined the authority of national leaders to maintain industrial peace. Labour sought to restore rank-and-file discipline, assuming that once discipline was restored, the Government could still use the advantage of familial relationships to work out peaceful, cooperative and effective collectivist relationships.

The Conservatives operated from a much gloomier view of their relationship with the trade union movement. Their governments had consistently failed to develop even the most superficial cooperation with the unions except when Walter Monckton, as Minister of Labour, followed Churchill's prescription to settle with the unions and preserve industrial peace at all costs. Conservative governments after that time discovered that the TUC almost enjoyed their incumbencies because the General Council could decide to refuse cooperation without suffering familial pressure or policy retaliation.[3] Moreover, occasional Tory-bashing was good for intra-union unity as well as for the prestige of individual union leaders. The TUC could vent all this intransigence confident that the post-war political bidding process would ensure that Conservative governments would continue to work for economic security.

Conservative purpose in 1970 was therefore quite different from Labour's in 1968. The Conservatives were less anxious to work out a cooperative relationship with the unions than to put that relationship on "automatic pilot". They proceeded with a two-part strategy. The first and most obvious was the reform of industrial relations. *Fair Deal at Work* was in the public domain for two years before the 1970 election and therefore politicians, trade unionists and civil servants, as well as the public, were well aware of its terms. The lines of disagreement were quite clear as the Heath Government took office in June.

The other part of the Conservative strategy was less obvious, though it could be gleaned from examining the statements of Tory leaders as well as from the Party manifesto of 1970.[4] The new Government planned to develop an economic policy which did not depend for its success on the approval, acquiesence or cooperation of the Trades Union Congress. Just as Heath hoped to put industrial relations on "automatic pilot", he equally hoped to avoid the traditionally intimidating interaction with the union movement which had so paralysed earlier Tory governments.[5]

TUC leaders fully recognized this Conservative threat; and the General Council was ready to fight back with much more relish than when it battled with the Wilson Government.[6] Its primary goal was the same: to preserve the basis and instrumentality for the influence which it had exerted on national economic policy-making over the previous two-and-a-half decades. Put more crudely, the General Council planned to force the Government to readopt Churchill's prescriptive warning to Monckton.

At the same time, though, the General Council was just beginning to recognize that it had another goal in the fight. High inflation was accompanied for the first time by high unemployment, which together challenged the conventional wisdom about how government might use economic policy to protect stability and well-being. The TUC economic staff warned that this new relationship required the TUC to do more than simply defend the *status quo*. The TUC during the seventies would need to win positive influence for policies which it felt would best protect working people's interests. It could no longer assume that the government would automatically provide that security by applying Keynesian theory.

I INDUSTRIAL RELATIONS

A.   PRELUDE TO CONFLICT

The battle between the Heath Government and the TUC thus shaped up as the most complex and significant of the collectivist era. The Government ran into trouble with both parts of its strategy from the beginning. Economic difficulties proved to be the most potent enemy, bolstered considerably by policies which were poorly constructed. The Government very quickly became fatally susceptible to the very collectivist relationship that it sought to end.

Industrial relations offers a good example of this process. *Fair Deal at Work* proved to be seriously flawed despite its tough and purposive tone. It suffered from technical flaws and even more from contradictions which only demonstrated that Tory leaders were considerably more uncertain about how to end their intimidating relationship with the union movement than they let on. The document imposed a framework of laws which can best be described as timid and at cross-purposes.

For example, *Fair Deal at Work*, as it was translated into legislation, both attacked the power of unions as collective organizations and tried to enhance the power of its national leadership.[7] Individuals were given the balanced right to join or not join unions. Unions were restrained at the same time in disciplining their members, and individual members were encouraged to complain about their union's misbehaviour to new legal institutions. The Government could act against industrial disruption by invoking a new emergency provision to get a strike ballot order from the

Industrial Relations Court, which would thereby give the union membership a chance to overrule its leadership.

On the other hand, the Act placed the full responsibility for industrial relations behaviour in the hands of the national union leadership, as opposed to the contemporary reality of that power being in the hands of shop stewards. In this regard, the Act provided for the registration of unions and for a registrar empowered to examine and influence the content of union rules. National union leaders were to be able thereby to act forcefully against rebellious local union organizations and ultimately conclude more effective national contracts.

But the Conservatives imposed these provisions only timidly. For example, unions could decide not to register. The Act did not make registration mandatory, as it might have done; it merely provided inducements and rewards in the form of tax advantages, etc., for those unions which did register. In the same way, the Act sought to bring collective agreements under the law but it provided an escape hatch for unions and employers by allowing them to agree that their contracts would not be legally binding.

The document was littered with such weaknesses, which are well analyzed in several studies.[8] Their effect was to weaken the Government's industrial weapon, making it susceptible to vigorous TUC opposition as well as industrial action from inevitably angry shop stewards. Conservatives quickly began to suffer at the hands of their own instrument.

The battle over industrial relations opened on 5 October 1970. Robert Carr, the Employment Minister, that day published his Consultative Document setting out the terms of legislation which the government planned to introduce.[9] The document proposed nearly all of the things which the unions had feared from their reading of *Fair Deal at Work*. This included, among other things: the registration of unions; compulsory and secret ballots; sixty-day cooling-off periods in certain strikes; a National Industrial Relations Court with legislative backing; a strengthened Commission on Industrial Relations with statutory powers; and a ban on the closed shop. Victor Feather had tried to head off the document in a conversation with Carr at the end of September.[10] He told the Minister that the Government was certain to find itself in a highly destructive conflict if it went ahead with its plans, but Carr would hear none of it. Carr also refused at the time to meet with the

General Council until after the Document was published.

That meeting finally occurred on 13 October. The General Council's inner group of senior leaders, the Finance and General Purposes Committee, met with both the Employment Secretary and Sir Geoffrey Howe. The atmosphere was already inflamed. Not only were union leaders angry about the Consultative Document, they were also embroiled in a fight against the Government's effort to impose an involuntary wage restraint in the public sector – a crucial part of the other half of the Conservative strategy to attack the collectivist relationship.

The meeting went quite badly.[11] Carr read a statement in which he told the TUC that there would be no negotiations about the eight central "pillars" on which the Document was based. Carr told union leaders that he would be happy to talk with them about the proposal, but that the discussions would have to be limited to the details of the recommendations. Moreover, he said that if the TUC participated in such talks, they must be completed within a month, with 13 November as the deadline.

Dismayed TUC leaders replied angrily. They had come to the meeting fully prepared to argue with Carr about his document. But they were appalled that he would try to bar them from discussing the central theses which underpinned his proposal.[12] The Minister's attitude thus finally confirmed for them that the Conservative Government was determined to exclude the trade union movement from its traditional bargaining position with government. Therefore, after warning him that he was mistaken if he thought he could impose a legal framework upon British industrial relations, the TUC delegation abruptly walked out of the meeting.

Once back at Congress House, Victor Feather ordered the TUC staff to move ahead with already developing plans for a public campaign against the Government's industrial relations policy. For the first time in the post-war era, relations between the union movement and the government were broken. Two years earlier the General Council had thought that the struggle over *In Place of Strife* might lead to such a break but the force of familial relations between the two wings of the Labour movement ultimately forestalled the rupture. But that cement was certainly lacking in 1970, both because of the difference in relationship between the Tories and unions and because the Heath Government was determined to break the traditional disadvantage of collectivist relations.

The General Council found it quite easy therefore to agree

unanimously to a public campaign. It was to be a massive and expensive advertising effort. The TUC would lead rallies, gather petitions against the bill, run media ads and generally work to educate the public and especially trade unionists about the threat that the bill posed to free collective activity. There would also be a series of regional and local meetings for union activists, climaxed by two rallies in London: a national rally at the Albert Hall in January followed by a mass rally at Trafalgar Square in February.

More militant leaders on the Council unsuccessfully suggested that the TUC should go even further. Hugh Scanlon, for example, proposed that the TUC should lead short general strikes and support various forms of local and regional industrial action.[13] The majority on the Council opposed this tactic vehemently because they worried that disruptions would only serve the Government's argument that its policy was necessary to keep the unions from ruining the country. Another moderate counter-argument was that the TUC would be most persuasive with public opinion if it could show that the Government's proposals were unreasonable and unnecessary, as well as undemocratic, since they sought to exclude the union movement from its legitimate activity as spokesman for Britain's working people.

The public campaign thus got under way immediately under moderate terms, though with the enthusiastic support of all activists in the union movement. Throughout the fall and winter of 1970–71, the campaign continued as the House of Commons considered the Industrial Relations Bill. Approximately one-third of the entire TUC membership, or about three million workers, participated in protest meetings, distributed literature, signed petitions or attended one of the many rallies.[14] The TUC spent £120,000 directly on the campaign, while its affiliated unions spent another £125,000.

A Special Trades Union Congress met on 18 March 1971 as the climax to the campaign. Its purpose was to decide how the trade union movement would respond to the impending Industrial Relations Act. The bill was nearing its third reading in the House of Commons and it was now clear that the bill would be completed and have its Royal Assent by the end of the summer.

Victor Feather stated the General Council's position, to which everyone could agree quite easily. The TUC's policy would be one of non-cooperation:

So in this Report to the Special Congress, the General Council rejects collaboration with the Government to try to make their legislation work. The General Council also reject any policy of encouraging unions and their members to commit deliberate breaches of the law. Instead, they are proposing to the Movement that it should adopt a policy of non-cooperation. By that, they mean that unions should refrain from availing themselves of any of the so-called advantages conferred by the Act; that they should avoid in every legitimate way the limitations that the Act seeks to impose upon unions; and that they should not lift a finger to facilitate the working of the bodies set up under the Act or any of the legislative purposes for which the Act provides.[15]

The debate at Congress on the package of General Council re-commendations showed that enthusiasm for the fight and resistance to the Act still remained at a very high level. At the same time, though, there was also evidence that the implementation of the Act would produce still further disagreement between moderates and militants about how far the TUC should push its opposition. The two great issues were whether the TUC should take a strong position against registering under the Act; and whether, as had been discussed by the Council earlier, the TUC should lead the movement in staging a barrage of industrial actions and other forms of disobedience.

Recommendation One strongly advised unions not to register under the Act, but raised the protest of militants by only mildy urging unions who felt they must register to first consult with the General Council. Jack Jones and Hugh Scanlon took the lead for the militants in arguing that this provision would inhibit the fight against the Act by diluting the unity that a policy of non-cooperation required.[16] Daniel McGarvey of the Boilermakers added in more acidic terms that the movement should not prepare an escape hatch "for those moderates who may want to find an avenue to capitulate".[17]

The sentiment of McGarvey, Scanlon, and Jones was that the new strength and unity that Victor Feather had fashioned the year before in order to find compromise with the Labour Government should now be used to strengthen confrontation with the Con-servatives. They pointed out that they had given up a portion of their authority to the TUC so that the TUC could act in the interest of the entire movement in monitoring unofficial strikes and the inflation of age claims. Now, they insisted, the time had come for the

TUC to use that authority to ensure the unity of the movement in the fight against the Government. If unions registered under the Act in opposition to TUC policy, they demanded that those unions be expelled from the TUC.

The other contentious General Council proposal was Recommendation Seven. Though innocuously worded, the recommendation rejected militant demands for industrial action as a tool in the fight against the Act. This question had been at issue in the General Council from the beginning of the public relations campaign in the early fall. Each time the General Council had considered a proposal for a national strike, the moderates had defeated the idea. The Engineers and a few other unions had nevertheless taken matters into their own hands, calling local and regional actions of short duration.[18] Now the issue came to a head at Congress, where the militants argued that the Government would never understand the resolve of trade unionists unless it faced the fire of strikes coupled with peaceful demonstrations. In response, Victor Feather restated the moderate position that strikes, whether national or local, short or long, would tend to undermine the public support which the TUC campaign had worked to build.[19] Feather told the Congress that industrial action would only play into the hands of those in the Government and among Tory politicians who were looking for further rationale in support of the legislation.

The moderate majority on the General Council was finally able to carry the day at the Special Congress. Five of the recommendations won unanimously. Numbers One and Seven scraped by with majorities of 800,000 and slightly more out of approximately 9 million votes cast. The militants nevertheless had shown their strength, which was a clear warning to the Council that it should lead the fight aggressively. In fact, six months later the 1971 regular Congress reversed its approval of the "soft" General Council policy on registration under the Act and approved a much tougher Scanlon-sponsored prescription.

Whatever disagreements about tactics though, there was a unity of enthusiasm about the struggle with the Tories. The contrast between the 1971 Special Congress and the 1969 Special Congress which dealt with *In Place of Strife* was striking indeed. The earlier Congress convened to help solve a family feud; the fight was not at all welcome and the outcome at that time was still very much in doubt. In 1971, the delgates could find considerable comfort in bashing the Tories and in prescribing action which they knew the union movement could do best: fighting the defensive battle against intrusive policies.

B. THE BATTLE AGAINST THE ACT: A SHORT FARCE

The Industrial Relations Act came into effect in stages from October 1971 up to the end of February 1972. The Trades Union Congress staff used the period after the Special Congress to develop specific plans for non-cooperation. Victor Feather personally worked very hard during this same period to maintain enthusiastic unity while restraining the passions of the more aggressive militants on the General Council. Feather expected a long fight, at least as long as the life of the government. He had learned in his contacts with those close to the Prime Minister that Heath was pinning his hopes for the success of the Act – that is, union compliance – on the force of public opinion and especially on rank-and-file trade unionists whom public opinion polls reported as being in favour of many provisions in the Act.[20]

The Prime Minister believed that this fundamental support would gradually force trade union leaders quietly to accept the Act over a period of two or three years.[21] It had been just this sort of optimism which had steeled Government strength to resist the TUC's earlier public relations campaign against the Bill.

The leaders of the main combatants in the battle over the Act therefore agreed at the outset that the fight would last for several years. But, in fact, the important battles were over and the Act lay in shambles within six months of the time that its last provisions came into effect. By August 1972 the Government had abandoned use of its own legislation and all but openly admitted that the project had been a failure. Edward Heath by that time was busy trying to woo the Trades Union Congress into a new collectivist relationship that would have made him wince only two years earlier.

The story of the collapse of the Act is a farce. Employers and individuals quickly showed the flaws in the Act's construction by initiating complaints that led to widespread and disruptive industrial actions. The economic situation deteriorated at the same time in a way which caused the Prime Minister to want closer relations with the unions. Employers colluded with the unions to circumvent some of the key purposes of the Act, such as their agreement to keep contracts outside the law. And most of all, the Trades Union Congress very efficiently operated its policy of non-cooperation, which left the Commission on Industrial Relations and sometimes even the National Industrial Relations Court in a near state of paralysis.

The net effect of the scenario was that the Government watched the disintegration of its plan to put relations with the union movement on "automatic pilot" while the force of disadvantageous collectivist relations re-emerged. This evolution was highlighted by a series of dramatic industrial conflicts beginning in March 1972.

Most of the incidents occurred on the docks and expressed the crisis of the continuing decline of employment in that industry, exacerbated by developing containerization. Trouble on the docks had simmered for a number of years.[22] Any real solution required long, tortuous and comprehensive bargaining between employers and the dockers, who are members of the Transport and General Workers Union. The Industrial Relations Act could not help this process because it could only be used against industrial actions and specific unfair practices such as the union blacking (boycott) of containers that hauliers loaded at their depots with non-docker labour. The Act not only failed to contribute to a solution, it exacerbated conflict by intruding poorly designed legal sanctions into a largely "political" situation. By doing so, the law itself became a mockery and the subject of conflict.

The first case involved a complaint by Heatons Transport to the National Industrial Relations Court that Transport and General Workers Union (TGWU) dockers in Liverpool were wrongly refusing to handle Heaton's containers.[23] The TGWU maintained TUC policy and refused to appear and defend itself before the Court. Heatons won the Court's order against further blacking. When the blacking continued, the Court first fined the TGWU £5000 and later added another £50,000. The main argument was about whether the TGWU was responsible for the discipline of its members. Certainly one of the Act's central purposes was to insist that national unions enforce their authority against unofficial strikes.

After the Court had meted out the second fine for contempt, the TUC reversed its policy and urged the TGWU to defend itself. It did so first in the NIRC and then up through the Appeal Court and finally to the House of Lords. Throughout, the TGWU maintained that it was not responsible for its members' behaviour, that it had never authorized the industrial action, and, moreover, that it had

attempted without success to end the blacking. Though the Appeal
Court found in favour of the TGWU and reversed the NIRC, the
House of Lords finally came down in favour of union responsibility;
and the fine stood. But the judgment had little effect on the issues
involved, and throughout the conduct of the case it was obvious that
the Act was wrongly directed in presuming that national union
leaders *could* discipline their membership. The four-week docks
strike that followed, compounded by other dock cases, showed that
the Act in truth was working against the development of more
peaceful industrial relations.

Other cases stirred passions even more. In the midst of the
Heatons dispute, in June 1972 three London dockers were ordered
to prison by the NIRC for refusing to cease their picketing of
container trucks from Chobham Farm terminal.[24] The dispute was
similar to Heatons except that the action was brought by depot
workers, themselves TGWU members from another section. Thus
the case involved the action of one section of TGWU members
against TGWU members from another section. Also, the depot
workers applied for and obtained an injunction against the three
workers and not against the union.

When subsequently the depot workers again complained to the
NIRC that the three workers were disregarding the injunction by
continuing to picket, the NIRC threatened to arrest the three unless
they appeared by 16 June at the NIRC or took the case to the
Appeal Court. The threat of arrest immediately sparked a sympathy strike by more than 30,000 dockers in several ports and there
were strong indications that there would be a total national strike to
follow if the arrests were carried out.

In what seemed a staged farce the Official Solicitor, Norman
Turner, headed off the crisis by suddenly and mysteriously taking
up the dockers' defence. The Court of Appeal accepted the Official
Solicitor's argument that there was insufficient evidence that the
three dockers had been contemptuous of the NIRC's injunction.
While everyone breathed a sigh of relief, there were widespread
rumours that the Government had intervened anonymously to head
off the imprisonment. The Master of the Rolls, Lord Denning,
denied the rumour. Denning insisted that he and his colleagues had
invited the help of the Official Solicitor at the Solicitor's suggestion.
About a week later, employers and union representatives resolved
the dispute by negotiation. The settlement provided that dockers
would work at the Chobham Farm terminal in the future though

the sixty-three non-dockers then employed would continue in their jobs.

Whatever the Government's involvement in staving off the jailing of the three dockers in the Chobham Farm case, it was to find itself involuntarily in more trouble with the Act almost immediately. Midland Cold Storage had brought an action against seven dock workers in early June and won an injunction against their blacking in another similar case.[25] Again, the dockers disobeyed the injunction and on 21 July the NIRC ordered that they be sent to Pentonville prison. The trade union movement responded immediately. Dockers staged a nationwide strike and were joined in sympathy by hundreds of thousands of workers in a large number of industries including newspaper, mining, automobile and road transport, among others.

The week of 23 July proved to be climactic in the struggle over the Industrial Relations Act. The Government that week fully recognized that the Act was a serious political liability, as well as technically flawed. Prime Minister Heath was by then most worried about solving the growing economic crisis.[26] The great uproar over the dockers' dispute and the strikes that followed not only threatened to do serious economic harm but forced even the moderates in the TUC leadership to turn their backs on discussion which Heath by then was anxious to begin.[27] Yet the Government had no mechanism by which it could intervene. The courts had the matter before them with the Pentonville Five jailed under its order. The system was working on "automatic pilot" just as the Tories had planned but now Heath needed a vehicle for political action. Still, everything had to await the court's actions and there was virtually nothing that negotiations could accomplish for the moment. Victor Feather's seemingly endless warnings about the harm that the Industrial Relations Act would do to traditional producer group–Government relations rang especially true. Ministers quietly rued the industrial relations policy which they had sold so forcefully to the electorate.

The TUC's Finance and General Purposes Committee met on Monday, 24 July to decide how to react to the mushrooming crisis. Later that same day they met at their request with the Prime Minister to urge that his Government quickly seek the dockers' release.[28] They reminded Heath that they had frequently warned that the Act would provoke just this sort of crisis. Moreover, they added that as matters stood they simply could not undertake further

discussions with the CBI and the Government about the management of the economy – not until the dockers were released.

But threats failed to budge the Prime Minister. He told them,
with a hint of exasperation, that as he had said before it was too soon
in the life of the Act to consider changes. He would be happy to
consider modifications at some future time, but not yet. And
besides, there was nothing he felt he could do about the jailed
dockers. There could be no question of interfering with the court's
work.

Members of the Finance and General Purposes Committee were
not surprised at Heath's position.[29] They had gone to see him as a
matter of protocol before they recommended that the General
Council call a one-day General Strike for the end of the week. They
had used the meeting as another opportunity to pressure the Prime
Minister to recognize the connection between his new-found
interest in resuming dialogue with the TUC and the political
liability of the Industrial Relations Act. Though some members
seemed to enjoy seeing the Prime Minister so harried, many others
worried that the crisis would radicalize the movement toward a no-
holds-barred conflict.

Heath had met with Carr, Macmillan, Home and Sir Geoffrey
Howe earlier the same day.[30] They had talked about emergency
plans including the possibility of using troops to unload perishable
cargo. They had also reached a consensus that the only hope for an
end to the crisis lay in two possible developments. First, as the
Secretary for Employment reported, there was the possibility that
the still unreleased Jones-Aldington Report on the docks situation
might provide the formula for general peace. Second, Sir Geoffrey
Howe reminded the group that the Law Lords would be soon
reporting their decision in the Heatons case and that the Lords
would almost certainly overturn the Court of Appeal's decision that
had exonerated the unions from responsibility. Such a reversal
would put responsibility back on to the unions and thus open the
way for the jailed workers to be released. But there was no firm
assurance about when the Lords would hand down their decision,
and there was no assurance that the dockers would accept the Jones-
Aldington recommendations, especially in the prevailing atmosphere.

The following day, 25 July, was a day of rising passions and
rumours.[31] At the TUC, the staff worked hard on plans for a
nationwide strike which the General Council would inevitably

sanction at its meeting the following day. Reports of new strikes poured in from around the country giving substance to the siege atmosphere. The largest industrial confrontation since the 1926 General Strike was clearly taking shape and there was a kind of heady confidence that the Government was finally getting the black eye it richly deserved and somehow had escaped during the long and costly TUC publicity campaign of the previous winter.

Meanwhile, there was new optimism in the Government as well.[32] Ministers heard that the Lords would give their judgment in the Heaton case the following day. Ministers also heard the rumour that the news would be "good", that the Lords would rule against the TGWU. But, even while the Ministers savoured the first good news in some days, there was renewed concern about the fate of future talks with the TUC. The Prime Minister's conversations with the Finance and General Purposes Committee seemed to threaten that this conflict, however or how soon resolved, might permanently alienate even moderate trade unionists.

The General Council met as scheduled on Wednesday, 26 July, and "enthusiastically" approved plans for a general strike to be held on 31 July. But later that same day, the Law Lords delivered the Government's "salvation" in the form of the expected decision reimposing responsibility (and therefore the £55,000 fine) on the Transport and General Workers Union. Five hours later the NIRC ordered the release of the five dockers on the grounds that the decision in the Heatons case established that unions are "primarily responsible for the wrongful acts of their shop stewards".[33] Michael Zander, writing in the *Guardian* two days later (28 July), wondered out loud about what had been going on behind the scenes that ultimately led to the dockers' release. After all, Zander pointed out, the "explanation given by the National Industrial Relations Court for the release of the five dockers was so manifestly defective that one is bound to ask whether the decision was in reality based on behind-the-scenes negotiations".[34] Zander, the *Guardian*'s legal correspondent, perceptively pointed out that the release "left completely unexplained how the Court could in good conscience release men imprisoned for contempt who remained totally unrepentant. The Law Lords' decision did nothing to remove the legal responsibility of individual shop stewards. . . . the only credible interpretation of what happened is that the Court, faced with a growing national crisis, capitulated to the necessity of releasing the dockers. Force of circumstances required the sacrifice of the rule of law at the risk of some lessening of respect for the courts."[35] Much as in the Chobham Farms case, there was wide speculation about the Lords' decision which so conveniently allowed the NIRC to release the dockers just when it looked as if there was to be a nationwide explosion of industrial conflict. There is no direct evidence of Government interference, and it is likely that the Government did not directly involve itself, just as the Prime Minister had told the Finance and General Purposes Committee on July 25. Rather, as the *Sunday Times* Insight team concluded, "the best verdict on the whole conspiracy theory came from the Communist Party's industrial organizer Bert Ramelson. 'There was no collusion,' he said, 'Just the needs of the ruling class to help each other.'"[36]

The release of the dockers from prison did avert the TUC's nationwide strike but the solution to the problems on the docks that caused the crisis remained more illusive. For a brief moment it looked as if the Government had found a solution for the dockers in the Jones-Aldington Report which had been issued on 24 July. However, a conference of docker delegates on 27 July demonstrated that their anger and distrust of the Government remained un-diminished.[37] By a vote of 38–28, they rejected the report and thus repudiated the recommendation of their own union leader, Jack Jones, as well as the urging of the TUC. With their industry in rapid decline, the delegates insisted on guarantees, not simply more inquiries and new schemes following in the parade of recom-mendations made since World War II. The Government therefore immediately faced a new nationwide dock strike instead of winning its formula for peace.

It was little noticed in all the confusion and excitement of this period that the Government itself stopped using its own Industrial Relations Act. The dockers' chaos was decisive for the Prime Minister, especially since it followed hard on some earlier un-pleasant first-hand experience. The Government had used the Act vigorously in the rail dispute during April 1972. It had gone to the NIRC for an order that the three rail unions cease their work slowdown and work-to-rule.[38] When the Court order failed to end the slowdown, the Government had returned to the NIRC for an order requiring a strike ballot. But the ballot proved to be a profound embarrassment, as the rank and file voted overwhelm-ingly to support their leaders.[39] Now, in July and August, the Prime Minister himself rejected further use of the Act.[40] He could have gone back to the NIRC to get an order requiring a strike ballot in the docks dispute, or threatened the imposition of a cooling-off period, or a declaration of national emergency. But he didn't because he worried that use of the Act would only inflame the situation still more; reasoning which was very close to the argument which Victor Feather had made to him privately on a number of occasions.

The Prime Minister had reached the point by this time that he would have been happy to amend the Act extensively.[41] However, he didn't feel he could go that far. The issue was too charged politically, with significant argument under way within the Conservative Party about what should be done. The Act had become an obvious embarrassment but the Party had become so committed to its purpose that there was widespread fear that its amendment would be enormously embarrassing. Also, the Labour Party had itself thrown down a challenge to Conservative resolve by reaching agreement with the TUC that the next Labour Government would immediately repeal the Act.

The Prime Minister did realize, however, that the Government might suffer further damage if it did nothing to change the Act. Individuals and employers could still operate the Act whether or not the Government used it. The dock strikes had grown from just this sort of action. Worse, Government failure to amend the Act followed by further crisis would obviously undermine what he regarded as a crucial effort to re-establish collectivist relations with the TUC.

This dilemma intruded hard into the negotiations that finally got under way between the TUC, CBI, and the Government in the summer of 1972. The Prime Minister tried to have his cake and eat it too. He staunchly preserved the Act, abandoning Government use of it, while he tried to do what no Tory Prime Minister had ever accomplished: reach some sort of cooperative relationship with the unions for wage restraint and the joint management of the economy.

II WAGE POLITICS

The reform of industrial relations was only one part of the new Conservative Government's strategy to do "something about the unions" as it took office in June 1970. The new Government also had plans to develop an economic policy which did not depend for its success on the approval, acquiesence, or cooperation of the Trades Union Congress.

Heath and his colleagues thus fitted their "union policy" into their larger plan to modify the terms of Conservative commitment to economic management. That commitment dated from the publication of the Tory *Industrial Charter* in 1947.[42] The Party after 1947 closed much of the distance between itself and Labour by pledging itself to follow a new course stressing the positive value of the state's management of the economy. While not renouncing Conservative commitment to manage the economy, Heath promised during the election campaign to identify and remove obstacles to growth. Government under the Tories would stress the development of the economy by competitive free enterprise. It would reduce its dependence on producer group relations for the success of its economic policies. Thus, in union–government relations, Heath promised the double-edged strategy of legislating an end to industrial chaos while avoiding the regular pattern of fruitless bargaining about incomes policy.

The TUC held the advantage in this fight. It marshalled its enormous power against the processes of change which Heath hoped would reduce that power. The TUC had shown this advantage in its struggle against *In Place of Strife* and the Industrial Relations Act. At the same time, the Government's broader strategy to deny the TUC so important a place in economic decision-making also suffered because the unions proved able to capitalize on Government's continued dependence on its cooperation during this period of economic difficulties. In the end, the TUC did beat back Tory efforts both to impose a framework of laws on British industrial relations and otherwise alter and reduce the power of unions in national economic decision-making.

These victories again demonstrated that the trade union movement has power to veto policies to which it objects. Yet these victories also raised new questions about whether the TUC could convert this awesome veto power into more positive influence on the terms of alternative economic policy. The changing nature of economic problems, especially the twin problems of high unemployment with high inflation, caused the TUC during the Heath years to take a more positive interest in what economic policies it wished the government to adopt. It was no longer sufficient in satisfying union concerns – as it had been for decades – for the TUC simply to deliver its veto against government policies it disliked and then leave the government alone to find some new policies which would fill the remaining vacuum. The experience of union–government relations during the Heath years provides evidence confirming the viability of union negative power as well as demonstrating its frustrating weakness in developing positive influence on policy-making.

A. TOWARD CONFLICT

Conservative plans to manage the economy without need of union cooperation were doomed from the moment the new Government took office. The economy was already suffering high price and wage inflation; there was no time, no "breathing space" during which the Government could even begin to affect fundamental and long-standing policy relationships. The Labour Government left a legacy of decontrolled wage bargaining with wage settlements approaching 20 per cent, and the annual rate of wage inflation at nearly 12 per cent.[43] At the same time, the number of unemployed was at a post-war high while unions continued to press wage demands in nationally sanctioned strikes involving large numbers of workers.[44] Only the balance of payments offered any cheer, still enjoying the devaluation-created surplus. But the fruits of that 1967 devaluation were showing signs of erosion as domestic inflation gradually destroyed Britain's international price advantage.

It was hardly surprising that only a few weeks after the new Government took office senior civil servants at the Treasury did indeed begin to warn the new Chancellor, Anthony Barber,[45] that Britain was heading for yet another period of economic trouble. By the middle of the summer of 1970 worried ministers agreed to detour from their original plan to develop a market economy in order to make an effort to regain control of the deteriorating situation.

The Cabinet in August after anguished discussion agreed that it would conduct a more interventionist policy. It continued to oppose a general incomes policy, still unpalatable in the wake of Tory election statements. But the cabinet did adopt an *indirect* incomes policy.[46] Under its plans, the public sector would serve as an example for the rest of the economy. Nationalized industries would still be free to bargain collectively with unions, but at their own risk. The Government no longer would "buy" industrial peace or in any way pay for inflationary settlements. The Cabinet also decided to "hang tough" in supporting this policy, even so far as suffering serious public sector strikes. Moreover, the policy would be dynamic: the government would press for progressively lower settlements, industry by industry (known popularly as the N-1 policy). By this example, the Cabinet hoped to convince the private sector to take up the battle so that individual concerns would gradually reverse the inflation of wage rates.

Barber, and the Employment Secretary, Robert Carr, initiated the Heath Government's relations with the TUC by explaining this policy to dismayed TUC representatives during August and September.[47] These meetings occurred just before Carr sent the TUC his Consultative Document proposing the terms of the Industrial Relations Bill. Though TUC leaders had waited uneasily to learn the new Government's intentions, they were alarmed by what they saw. Their first reaction was to launch a strong effort to convince the Government that its plans would lead inevitably to conflict with the union movement; that instead, the Government should stick to traditional collectivist dialogue.[48] Trade union leaders told Carr and Barber that though they understood the argument in favour of wage restraint, three years of just-ended voluntary and statutory restraint made it necessary that their members enjoy a period of free bargaining during which they could restore important pay differentials and regain some of the losses in their standard of living.[49] They also warned the Government against exaggerating the role of rising wages in producing general inflation. Inflation, they argued, was due more to rising unit costs created by Britain's stagnant productivity. The remedy, in the TUC's view, was reflation and investment, not the dogmatic restriction of wage increases.

These early contacts produced no more than a superficial exchange of views. The Cabinet, at this point, remained studiously committed to its position, which included avoiding anything which even hinted at negotiations with the TUC. In reality, therefore, while the Trades Union Congress opened its public relations campaign against the Industrial Relations Bill, it also opened a union-by-union struggle against the N-1 incomes policy in the public sector.

Heath, Carr and Barber, who took the lead in policy-making that most concerned union interests, hoped to avoid conflict. But they were willing to risk conflict in order to win their plans to restructure industrial relations and manage the economy more as they saw fit. Moreover, they recognized that the conflict might indeed provide political dividends by demonstrating that their Government was the first in post-war history to stand up to the unions, just as Conservatives had promised during the election.

The union side had mixed feelings. Conflict with the Tories had traditionally helped to unify the union movement, and renewed unity at this point would be welcome in the wake of years of tension between national union leaders and the militant shop stewards movement. Yet the disadvantage of conflict with the new Government was that the TUC would be in a weak position to press their criticisms and alternative policy proposals to deal with the very real economic problems which the Government was beginning to address. In the end, the TUC General Council decided reluctantly. to boycott further talks with Robert Carr about his Consultative Document because it seemed to the Council that the Government was bent on excluding the union movement from its traditional and rightful influence.[50] The struggle, wanted or not, seemed inevitable.

Events worked in the TUC's favour over the months between the fall of 1970 and the late winter of 1972. Not only did the Industrial Relations Act work badly, but the struggle over the indirect incomes policy, after first signals had shown otherwise, dramatically turned against the Government. Even more importantly, the economic situation gradually forced the Government back toward collectivist policies. Unemployment, high inflation, and other problems touched sensitive political nerves within the Heath Cabinet that undermined economic innovation. Gradually, Heath took a new interest in developing discussion and cooperation with the trade union movement. The elements that produced and then nurtured collectivist politics after the war reasserted themselves during the first half of the Heath Government's incumbency, despite all Tory hopes to the contrary.

B. THE WAGE BATTLE IN THE PUBLIC SECTOR

The struggle over incomes policy in the public sector raged throughout 1971 and into 1972. The electricity workers and then the postal workers staged the first key battle of this period in early 1971. Over the same period, the unemployment rate leaped by about 50 per cent, sparking intense debate about the conduct of economic policy.[51] The popular assessment of the Conservatives' first year in office at the middle of 1971 was that the government was winning the wage battle but losing the economic war.

The electricity workers stirred fleeting predictions that the Government would soon abandon its N–1 policy.[52] They made the British winter exceptionally bleak at the beginning of 1971 by refusing to work overtime and by working to rule. They insisted that they be treated as an exception to official policy. They argued that they had received raises only half of those gas workers had won since 1969; which they believed was especially unfair because during the same period they had made significant contributions to productivity. But they saw no alternative to making their claim by industrial action because the Conservative Government failed to allow for special cases in their *de facto* wage restraint policy.

A Committee of Inquiry under the chairmanship of Lord Wilberforce condemned the dispute after power shortages had created significant industrial disruption. The final settlement generally favoured the union position although the Government took comfort in interpreting the terms as fully within its guidelines. But whether within the policy or not, the Government did resolve the conflict by refusing to consider the merits of the electricity workers' arguments. For the union movement, the electricity dispute demonstrated again that the Government was aggressively hostile.

The postal workers followed the electricity workers in the pay queue, pressing what they believed was their own good cause for special treatment.[53] Again, the Government's intransigence tended to radicalize the postal workers to press industrial action at an early point in the dispute. But the postal workers were considerably less cohesive than the power workers. Thus, the Government could score a decisive victory by holding firm, giving the impression that it was winning its policy.

The postal strike lasted for more than a month and a half. Mail tie-ups did indeed cause economic disruption. Yet the mail strike was not nearly as damaging as the power dispute because other communication branches of the postal union ignored the strike, even helping to facilitate alternative means of contact. Moreover, the union lacked the strike fund it needed to sustain its members over a very long period. Even so, Tom Jackson, the postal workers' leader, might still have done better if he had been able to win the financial support of other TUC unions.[54] But despite official TUC cheers, no other unions gave strike funds to the postal workers and only a few loaned funds. Even the loaned money fell far short of what Jackson needed and eventually he gave up the fight, winning only a promise that a committee of inquiry would investigate the dispute. The final settlement reached in May 1971 provided for a 9 per cent increase in wages, which was far below both what the Postal Union had demanded and what the electricity workers had won earlier.

This virtual humiliation of the postal workers proved to be an important benchmark in the public-sector wage struggle. From that point on until the end of 1971, other settlements fell within the same range. The Government seemed to be winning its policy. Just as impressive, the number of strikes and workers involved in stoppages declined dramatically.[55] The widely-held impression, in good measure shared at Congress House, was that the union movement had become worried, subdued and somewhat pessimistic about its prospects for defeating hated Tory policy. Even the more vocal and militant leaders spoke less optimistically about making gains against the Tories. The gloom at Congress House, at the same time, also proceeded from the worsening unemployment problem. During the previous two years, the number of unemployed had fluctuated between 500,000 and 600,000.[56] In January of 1971, the number jumped to 671,000 and four months later to well over 700,000. By August it had topped 800,000 without signs of reaching its peak.

The surge in unemployment acted as a siren for the union movement. The TUC in its economic reports of 1971 and the year before had paid special attention to the problem of unemployment.[57] Also, in their meetings with the new Government, TUC representatives had at every opportunity stressed its recommendations that there be an immediate reflation sufficient to head off the sort of rise in unemployment which by then had become a reality. The Government's response each time was to acknowledge concern about unemployment but stress the danger of inflation in its policy decisions.[58] The TUC felt extremely discouraged therefore because the Government's intransigence reinforced by conflict had to that point successfully excluded TUC influence – at a time when the union movement had substantive plans it hoped the Government would adopt.

Yet, at this moment when the Government seemed to be gaining the upper hand, the very same issue of unemployment began to cause significant concern in the Cabinet. Conservatives also suffered from a special sensitivity about unemployment. Despite Conservative commitments to the post-war economic contract which promised full employment as government's first priority, it seemed

that the electorate generally accepted Labour's charge that the
Tories held Darwinian contempt for the problem of employment.
Tories had long accepted that Churchill lost the 1945 election
because the public doubted Tory resolve to deliver economic
security. Moreover, they recognized that fear of unemployment was
burnt deep into the British psyche and that the rising unemployment of 1971 was producing easily the greatest stir in those feelings
since the end of the war.

C. TENTATIVE STIRRINGS OF COLLECTIVIST POLITICS: 1971

The unemployment question thus gradually forced the Government to reassess its economic strategy and its relationship with the
TUC at a time when the success of the Industrial Relations
legislation in moving through Parliament and the Government's
comparative successes in the public-sector wage fight would have
made change unlikely. Ministers met with the TUC in this context
for the first time in March 1971. The meeting formally was part of
an annual series of discussions between the incumbent Chancellor
and the TUC Economic Committee for the purpose of examining
the TUC's annual *Economic Review* before the Chancellor delivered
his budget.

The meeting that year was attended by the full General Council
and by Prime Minister Heath, leading a complement of senior
ministers including the Chancellor, the Secretary for Employment
and the Secretary for Trade and Industry.[59] The discussion, or
perhaps it should be styled the argument, primarily dealt with the
issues of economic growth, inflation, and especially unemployment.
In many ways, the discussions were similar substantively to those
between the Chancellor and the TUC during the previous summer.
The TUC again insisted that wage inflation was not the root cause
of the general inflation. Rather, the TUC continued to argue that
the stagnation of demand had produced an excessively high unit
cost and that a general reflation of demand at home was necessary
for the revitalization of business investment as well as trade union
cooperation in improving the very low level of productivity.

In reply, the Prime Minister took the lead for the Government in
restating his views, which stressed expansion: the Government
remained committed to growth as a major priority. But the Prime
Minister also argued that while expansion would certainly help to
improve unit costs, it was wage inflation that really caused rises in

unemployment. The possibility that growth could bring down unemployment depended on reducing wage inflation in order to protect the balance of payments. Government, unions, and management, he insisted, would need to cooperate in order to improve real wages, investment, and productivity. Thus, although the Government was not in favour of an incomes policy *per se*, it was very aware that "the problem of wage inflation was the major single constraint preventing a policy of expansion".[60]

This 11 March meeting did little to bridge the distance between the two sides but the meeting did importantly demonstrate to both parties that they held similar concerns that pressing economic problems be tackled quickly. The rising unemployment rate worked as a catalyst, while the problem of how to deal with inflation remained the bone of contention. While the TUC's substantive proposals were not taken up by the Chancellor in his late March budget, the TUC did take considerable encouragement from the Chancellor's promise to stimulate growth more aggressively if his mild reflationary package proved inadequate.

Contact between the Government, the CBI and the TUC became routinized during the spring and summer through the National Economic Development Council (NEDC). At this point, none of the parties wanted publicly to be seen being too conversational with each other. The TUC was still in full battle against the Industrial Relations Act and the indirect incomes policy. The Government worried that full-scale, public conversation with the TUC would anger and demoralize its supporters, who were just then basking in the Government's apparently successful "union bashing" strategy. All agreed therefore that they would talk at regular Neddy meetings and through the good offices of the Director-General, Fred Catherwood.

Victor Feather was especially pleased by the developing contact with the Government.[61] Feather had led the demonstrations against the Industrial Relations bill and was certainly appalled at the Government's *de facto* wage policy in the public sector. But he was increasingly anxious as the spring wore on that the TUC should urgently develop as much positive influence with the Government as possible. The trade union movement, he believed, simply could not afford to boycott contact with the Government because there were important interests that the TUC needed to protect.[62] The unemployment issue was easily the most obvious and the most vital. Moreover, Feather was also convinced that the Government wanted to preserve the relationship. Whatever their bluster on incomes policy, he was sure that at some point they would want consensual dialogue. It would be at that moment that the TUC, he believed, must be in a position to take advantage of the opportunity. The Chancellor's budget speech provided such an opportunity and Feather, for one, was busily working privately to develop his and the TUC's influence.

Discussions continued from May until July 1971 in the NEDC.[63] In early July, the TUC offered a summary of its views in an extensive paper on inflation, economic growth, and unemployment. While the TUC position was not materially different from the views it expressed at the March meeting, it did put far greater stress on tripartite cooperation in removing the obstacles to growth. Even the question of wages, the TUC pointed out, could be included in the larger discussion on the future conduct of the economy which it suggested should be coordinated through the NEDC:

> Under the auspices of NEDC there must, therefore, be a real attempt to secure an area of common understanding about what each party can contribute, and is or is not in a position to deliver. The headings of the agenda for such discussions are implicit in the TUC's approach, but it is not for the TUC to determine the final outcome unilaterally any more than it would be for the CBI or the Government to do the same. But the TUC representatives are ready to co-operate on tripartite discussions on the basis outlined above.[64]

The conciliatory and cooperative tone set by the TUC paper and the discussions in the NEDC did encourage both the Government and the CBI to take specific policy action in the hope of encouraging the TUC to go further. On 15 July, the CBI, after bilateral consultations of its own with the Government, announced that it would ask its membership to do everything possible over the following twelve months to keep price increases to 5 per cent or less. The President of the CBI announced that he would seek written agreement for this policy from about 200 of Britain's largest firms. Four days later, on 19 July, the Chancellor announced a more significant reflation of the economy.[65] His statement proceeded from an admission that the level of industrial output in the first half of the year was a full 1 per cent below what he had assumed in presenting his budget. Therefore, he said, new public spending coupled with further tax concessions were appropriate in order to stimulate faster growth.

The Chancellor concluded his statement to the House of Commons with an explicit reference to the Trades Union Congress. He hoped that the TUC could now examine how it could best make a contribution to economic stability, now that the Government had made good its pledge to move against unemployment and a stagnating economy, coupled with the CBI's initiative on prices.[66]

Replying through the press, Victor Feather welcomed the Chancellor's "change of heart" and his fast response to the TUC proposals which were offered at the NEDC.[67] While the new policies would be only a first step in reducing unemployment, they would be helpful. As for the problem of wage inflation, Feather saw "no basis for apprehension that a reduction in unemployment will stimulate wage claims".[68] In fact, he thought that "these measures will help encourage negotiation of cost of living threshold agreements".[69]

Sir Sidney (now Lord) Greene, chairman of the TUC Economic Committee, repeated the General Secretary's conciliatory position in early September at the TUC Congress. Greene also re-emphasized the scheme for threshold agreements which the TUC had first proposed in its 1971 *Economic Review* and again proposed in its NEDC paper. Greene told the Congress that:

> On the wages/prices front, trade union members fully recognize the futility of negotiating high money increases only to have these immediately swallowed up by rising prices. That is one of the reasons why the TUC has proposed the negotiation of "cost-of-living threshold agreements". Such agreements would mean that, in order to limit the immediate wage increase, a further increase would become payable if the cost of living rose by a certain amount within a given period. This proposal is anti-inflationary in that it is directed at one of the crucial difficulties in the wage/price spiral, namely that people anticipate its continuing.[70]

The threshold proposal was taken up in the NEDC during the autumn and became the subject of an NEDC study. Little became of the idea immediately, primarily because the Government and the CBI remained uncertain about the consequences of threshold agreements and somewhat suspicious that such agreements would simply lock in increases which would work as add-ons to more

traditionally reached annual wage increments. But neither side ever
rejected the idea and a year later it reappeared on a government
proposal in full-scale negotiations about incomes policy.

The dialogue in 1971 did not produce any substantive cooperation but these contacts did serve to show that all sides held a stake in
re-establishing substantive contact. The moves by the Government
and CBI were very positive from the TUC's point of view since they
were in the direction of reflation and price control. There was still
little evidence that the TUC really had made specific impact by its
argument or that the Government was acting in expectation of
TUC reciprocity on wages, though the Government certainly
would have welcomed such a move. This period of dialogue was also
important because it marked a turning-point for the Heath
Government. The Government explicitly acknowledged its concern
and interest in solving the problem of unemployment, as compared
to its earlier stress on solving inflation and heading off threats to the
balance of payments. By making this change, by opening and
furthering relations with the unions, the Government also moved at
least in the direction of collectivist-dependent policies which it had
earlier vigorously rejected.

D. THE 1972 MINERS' STRIKE: SHOCK TREATMENT FOR THE HEATH GOVERNMENT

The dialogue with the Government and the CBI in the NEDC was a
very favourable development from Victor Feather's point of view.
But the 1971 Congress hardly celebrated or perhaps even noticed
this development as it went about its business of excoriating the
Government of the day. As an example of hostility, few Congresses
in TUC history displayed any harsher feelings about the persons
and the policies of a Tory or Labour Government. The Industrial
Relations Act had just become law and bargaining in the public
sector industries had gone very badly after the postal strike was
settled on essentially Government terms. But for Victor Feather and
other key leaders, including moderates such as Sir Sidney Greene
and Alfred Allen, the TUC was at least moving in the direction
toward being able to exercise some influence on the Government.

In this hopeful context, the TUC leadership therefore viewed the
developing struggle in late 1971 between the miners and the
Government with some alarm.[71] Feather and his more moderate
colleagues together with even a few leaders on the left were not

anxious to start a new round of confrontation. With the Industrial Relations Act just then coming into effect, and the number of unemployed at more than one million, it seemed important to nurture communication and encourage a continued return to influence if possible. A miners' strike looked like a dangerous adventure. While the miners might make the Government uncomfortable, TUC leaders generally viewed their potential for success as slight – probably their chances being only slightly more than the postal workers. But TUC concern for moderation was not shared by the miners, who struck for the first time since the General Strike of 1926. And the TUC turned out to be very wrong in its calculation of the miners' effectiveness.

The miners defeated the Government in early 1972 by displaying tenacious unity in demanding that they be considered for special treatment.[72] The strike lasted seven weeks and was particularly savage and effective. Miners not only stopped production of coal, they stopped delivery of coal and other important materials to power generating plants. While the miners' leaders, Joe Gormley and Lawrence Daly, argued the miners' case in the media, the public began to feel and then to be hurt from severe power disruptions.

The arguments made by the union leaders were telling.[73] Their plea for special consideration made the Government appear harsh and inflexible in the operation of its public-sector incomes policy. The miners argued that their union had contributed voluntarily over more than a decade to the running down of the coal industry. There were then less than 300,000 miners still employed, compared to the more than 700,000 only a decade earlier. All of this sacrifice had produced vastly increased productivity in the industry. But for their effort, they could point out that the pay of those miners still on the job had fallen well behind workers in manufacturing industries. What miners wanted now, their leaders urged, was only a fair reward for their sacrifices and a wage that was reasonably comparable to what they had earned ten years earlier.

In the end, the Government was saved again by Lord Wilberforce, with a recommendation for a 20 per cent increase in pay.[74] The miners, at the last moment, did hold out for a bit more and the strike finally came to an end in late February. But the Government, which could have earlier agreed to consider the miners a special case, suffered the indignity of having that view forced on them by a long and damaging strike. Even more importantly, the miners' strike shattered the Government's incomes strategy. A few months later, the railwaymen struck a final blow at the policy.[75]

E. TRIPARTISM, 1972

The miners' strike was a watershed marking the beginning of the end of the Government's confrontation policy over public sector wages; in reality, a *de facto* wages policy. The strike was also a severe blow to the broader government strategy to change the British pattern of collectivist politics. Though it was not until the summer of 1972 that the Industrial Relations Act collapsed into disrepute in the wake of the docks uproar, the Prime Minister admitted as early as February 1972 that "We have to find a more sensible way of settling our differences."[76]

Throughout the spring of 1972 and especially after the Government floated the pound in late June, the Prime Minister took up his own advice and pressed the TUC to agree to open talks about the management of the economy. Heath's sharp turn toward collectivism was greeted as a welcome sign of victory at the TUC. The government seemed to have learned that it could not avoid considering the interests and power of the trade union movement either in economic politics or industrial relations. TUC leaders believed that trade unionism had won back its rightful place at the centre of economic decision-making. They also believed that they stood at the zenith of their power and influence during that summer of 1972.

This important victory posed both opportunity and dilemma. The General Council clearly recognized that like the Government, the union movement held an important stake in solving Britain's increasingly serious economic problems. High inflation together with high unemployment was a dangerous combination for British working people, made more frightening by the Government's now more uncertain commitment to the terms of the 1944 all-party agreement on economic security, especially the commitment to full employment. The Prime Minister's urging for collectivist negotiations thus offered the TUC a golden opportunity to use its new strength to press for remedial policies which would place special emphasis on restoring full employment and freezing price levels.

But this opportunity for influence and, as Heath offered later in the talks, for having a share in the management of the economy, injected a new element of tension into the General Council. It quickly became apparent that the possibility of cooperating with a Tory Government, however potentially rewarding in policy terms, would produce conflict and fissures between factions of union leaders. This effect was almost precisely the reverse of the effect that conflicts with the Tories had produced during the first two years of the Heath Government. The struggle against the Industrial Relations Act and the *de facto* wage policy in the public sector had created new unity while ending the long struggle between national union leaders and their shop stewards movement. Now cooperation with the Tories threatened to destroy that unity.

Militant and moderate leaders finally agreed to join the talks in mid-July but only after serious argument. The mediating efforts of the General Secretary, Victor Feather, prevailed.[77] Feather convinced the Council that the TUC had everything to gain and nothing to lose from talking with the Government. The TUC certainly had no need to reach agreement at the end unless the Prime Minister was prepared to accept TUC terms which would give the union movement substantial policy gains. Feather argued persuasively that the TUC had won its chance to put those terms to the Government and therefore had no need to continue to "shout" its views from a distance. While he recognized that the Tory Government had shown itself to be a dangerous adversary, the General Council should, as a matter of self-interest, test Heath's offer of influence on policy-making which the unions had so powerfully earned by their struggles.

The more militant members of the General Council reluctantly agreed to go along with the talks on this basis.[78] But they made it clear that they were opposed to reaching agreement with Heath on any terms short of the Government's unqualified acceptance of TUC proposals. Moreover, they wanted no part of the Prime Minister's offer to include the TUC in a permanent triumvirate which would manage the economy. They were determined to protect the free bargaining process. They were also determined to protect the voluntary system of industrial relations which they believed they had earned by their struggles first against *In Place of Strife* and then the Industrial Relations Act. They were completely unwilling, therefore, to submit to what they believed was a Tory strategy to win by stealth what they could not force by confrontation.

The talks opened on 18 July in the National Economic Development Council (NEDC). TUC negotiators from the beginning could do no more, therefore, than play out their role with mock seriousness.[79] Without near unanimity in the General Council, there was virtually no chance that they could conclude any sort of agreement with this Government. The TUC delegation represented nearly every segment of opinion within the trade union movement. Besides Victor Feather, the delegation included moderates Sir Sidney Greene, Alfred Allen and Lord Cooper, together with Jack Jones and Hugh Scanlon, who spoke for more militant elements and represented the TUC's largest unions.

The media largely failed to consider this intra-union political argument in their reporting and speculations about the possible success of these talks during the summer and fall of 1972. Instead, journalists focused on the jousts between the TUC, the CBI, and the Government over, first, the question of whether there would be talks and then, once talks began, about the details of the various counter-proposals. They mistakenly took heart from the fact that negotiations continued, assuming that the chances for some sort of agreement rested primarily on compromising the differences over the terms of wage and price controls.[80]

The Prime Minister and his colleagues operated from the same misconceptions.[81] Heath had always believed that rational men could reach rational agreements, but Victor Feather encouraged the Prime Minister in private conversations at Number 10 to apply that belief to these talks. The TUC delegation lent apparent serious interest in negotiating. The profound disagreements within their ranks went largely unnoticed, with the Prime Minister tending to believe that properly-stated militant objections to the talks would not be allowed to interfere with the apparent new TUC interest in exploring tripartite cooperation.

The TUC Congress reinforced both this illusion and the reality of intra-union disagreement. By the time that Congress opened in early September, the tripartite negotiators were deeply immersed in discussions about pay and prices. Working groups were studying both issues and promised to report by the middle of September. The Government feared Congress would openly rebel against its leaders participating in the talks.[82] But when Congress passed a relatively mild and contradictory resolution criticizing Government policy in only the most general terms and without mentioning the talks,[83] the Cabinet viewed the rebuke as an optimistic signal.

What the Government did not perceive were the private

meetings held at Congress where members of the General Council heard clear warnings that their own misgivings about a deal with the Tories were shared widely both by other union executives as well as by the shop stewards' movement.[84] The possibility of a share in economic management was clearly not sufficient incentive for agreement. The widespread feeling at Congress was that the unions needn't "buy" participation in economic decision-making because they had already earned that right by their struggles over the last half-decade, confirmed by the Prime Minister's urgent invitation for the TUC to join the talks.

Events at Congress, therefore, had great impact, albeit in contradictory ways, on the negotiations which resumed on 14 September at Chequers. The Government believed that the union side would now be free to negotiate from a "realistic" position, rather than from the posturing, maximal stance it had so far adopted.

The TUC team, by contrast, now fully accepted that the tripartite talks would fail. Union negotiators, in the main, expected to work to salvage the best possible public image. There was, of course, always the possibility that the Government would become so desperate for agreement that it would yield concessions beyond the TUC's wildest dreams. But short of this nearly irrational possibility, the talks would fail because trade union leaders were not prepared to sacrifice their own internal trade union standing by reaching an agreement with this Tory Government. Thus, suffering from its misperceptions, the Government during the balance of the talks waited to learn the minimum union position. The unions did in fact offer their minimum position but the Government could never believe that their price could be so "unrealistically" high.

Negotiations resumed in this context with all apparent serious-ness once Congress had ended. The working party on pay and prices had in fact proceeded energetically while the general sessions were in recess during Congress. The "group of four", as the working party came to be known, consisted of Victor Feather for the TUC, Campbell Adamson for the CBI, Sir William Armstrong for the Government and Sir Frank Figgures, the Director-General of NEDC. They reported to a general meeting on 14 September that they were making more progress on pay than on prices.[85] The major approach on pay was towards across-the-board flat-rate increases accompanied by incentive schemes with attention to the problem of lower-paid workers and the possibility of adopting threshold agreements. On prices, the group drew attention to the possibilities of Government action to lower the VAT tax, to postpone rent increases due in April 1973, and to impose controls on certain food and on rises in prices charged by nationalized industries. The working unit also reported that they could not agree on several other TUC proposals. These included proposals about EEC food prices, as well as the probability of controls on credit as well as house and land prices.

Twelve days later, on 26 September, the Prime Minister offered the Government's first comprehensive proposal based on the working group's report.[86] Heath suggested a tripartite approach to the management of the economy. The Government would agree to do everything necessary to develop a 5 per cent per year growth rate over the following two years in order to rebuild national prosperity and reduce unemployment. Employers should agree, he said, to accept the same 5 per cent figure as the upper limit for price increases; nationalized industries would do the same. Unions, for their part, should accept a pay rise limit of £2 per week over the next 12 months, with no rise effective less than one year after the previous increase. To ensure that potential inflation did not cause such a pay restraint to impose hardships, Heath proposed a TUC-originated system of threshold payments, with wages to rise by 20 pence for each 1 per cent above the threshold of 6 per cent. "Finally, pensioners would not only gain by the reduced level of inflation but the Government promised to take 'appropriate action to ensure that in the coming year pensioners also had the benefit of a share in the nation's increasing prosperity'."[87]

These proposals were, as Eric Jacobs said later in his inquest into the talks, "bold and simple in outline".[88] Heath believed that his proposals would succeed because they satisfied the demands made by both sides, especially the unions. Victor Feather had contributed importantly to Heath's optimism in private talks. Feather had not negotiated with Heath during these sessions but he had explained the union position and otherwise helped in guiding the Prime Minister in what he believed would be the most fruitful direction.[89] Heath also believed that Feather had at least indirectly signalled that the General Council would accept a deal if the terms were right.[90]

These private talks served unfortunately to add to misconceptions, especially for the Prime Minister. During the *In Place of Strife* controversy, Feather had frequently met with Wilson, Castle and the others in the search for compromise. The familial relationships mixed with often brutally frank exchanges produced fruitful dialogue. But in his conversations with Heath, Feather tended to be less frank, especially when discussing the "family matter" of intra-union problems. He gave more generalized advice which was open to speculation. While Feather did get on quite well with Heath,[91] there remained an intangible but important distance. Moreover, the two men tended to avoid intractable issues, such as the widespread demand from within the union movement that the talks produce a change or repeal of the Industrial Relations Act. Without baring those issues, it often seemed to Mr Heath that it would be possible for rational men to work out nearly any problem.[92]

The TUC Economic Committee considered the Prime Minister's proposals. Its response foretold the course of the negotiation. The Committee complained that the Government was promising too low a growth rate – 6 per cent would be far better. Also, the TUC calculated that the pay arithmetic should have been done on a different basis, providing for a rise of £3.40; and that price controls should be far more stringent, detailed and perhaps statutory than the Government was suggesting. The response discussed a wide variety of issues, stating disagreement with the Government at nearly every point. But again the Government and media found encouragement.[93] Both took heart especially from the difference of less than a point between the negotiators on the pay issue. They noticed less TUC objections to other issues which they believed would yield to further talks, especially dissolving when the TUC put its minimal demands on the table. Yet the real significance of the TUC response was that the TUC checklist of objections added up to a quantity of issues, any one of which could and *would* be used as the basis for forcing the talks to end in failure.

Further progress on the pay issue at the 16 October meeting continued to mask the TUC intransigence, particularly about price controls. But on 26 October and at the three following meetings the price issue came to the fore as discussion broadened to deal with the whole concept of what would constitute a mutually acceptable package arrangement.[94] The argument focused on TUC insistence that prices be strongly "guaranteed" by the Government not to rise more than 5 per cent. The TUC insisted that the Prime Minister had been too vague about the target figure in his proposal. If workers were to agree to specific and solid pay limits, then, the TUC argued, prices should be equally pegged and backed by legislation which would be effective for at least the next twelve months.

In talks on 30 October, the Government offered new concessions, providing strengthened voluntary price controls.[95] Ministers emphasized that a voluntary system of price controls was the only equitable accompaniment of the voluntary system of pay restraint being asked of the TUC. Price restraint was not only to include manufactured goods at 4 per cent over the next 12 months, but also to include prices set by the nationalized industries. The Government added that a large number of retail grocers were willing to set maximum prices for certain foods and not to increase their margin on other goods by more than 5 per cent without the approval of a monitoring body.

Despite the fresh proposals, the meeting ended without further movement toward agreement. The TUC argued that the new proposals on prices were still not strong enough to warrant the sort of commitment being asked of workers about their pay.[96] The Prime Minister replied that there could not be a double standard. There must be either voluntary agreements covering both prices and wages, or equally stringent legislation. He called on the TUC to indicate which approach it favoured. The TUC representatives in conclusion agreed to review the question with the General Council.

The negotiations were clearly at a climactic point, as the TUC team recognized that the Government side was losing its patience. There was no doubt that if the TUC refused to come to terms, the Government intended to legislate statutory restraints and certainly withdraw the Prime Minister's offer of joint management of the economy. The General Council therefore considered whether these threats should cause it to reverse its earlier view that the talks must end in failure.

The Council's answer was an emphatic "No!" The Government had obviously not "caved in" to TUC terms and therefore agreement with the Tories still posed overwhelming danger. The advice heard at Congress as well as the long-standing argument between militants and moderates within the Council could not be ignored. The reality of internal union politics argued that cooperation with the Conservatives would prove divisive within the union movement, whereas continued intransigence would probably continue to be beneficial. In short, then, it seemed better to give up the possibility of a formal share in economic management, to let the Tories legislate their wage and prices policy, however distasteful, than to chance the taint of collaboration.

The General Council based their formal response to the Prime Minister on this decision to avoid agreement. The response was carefully worded to meet criticism that the TUC was sabotaging the talks; only a few days earlier the Government and the CBI had attempted to mount pressure on the TUC by using a "blame strategy" through the media. Therefore, the TUC tactically offered a counter-proposal that at first glance appeared to take a con-ciliatory approach but showed, on closer examination, to be a harder position than it had taken earlier.[97]

The TUC's reply narrowed its demands, focusing on the price of food and rents. It was in this area, the General Council argued, that its members spent more than half of their income. "It is not practicable for the General Council to consider a policy on pay – particularly a policy which is as specific as that which is being proposed – if there are no guarantees on these two critical features, food and rents."[98] Then, in the last paragraph, the General Council reminded the Government that it still insisted that there be policy concessions on housing and taxation, property incomes, on pen-sions, the poverty trap, and the "non-operation of the Industrial Relations Act".[99]

The Prime Minister, on 1 November, complained that the General Council's new statement completely ignored his question of whether the TUC would prefer statutory or voluntary controls on both pay and price. In reply, Victor Feather and the other TUC negotiators strongly insisted that the Prime Minister was mistaken; the General Council, they said, had dropped its insistence on statutory price controls in favour of accepting a Government "guarantee". That will not do, Heath retorted. He wanted to know then if the TUC was prepared to continue to talks, recognizing that the Government and the CBI remained committed either to an all-voluntary or an all-statutory policy.[100] Sir Sidney Greene said the TUC would continue and wait to hear the Government's reply to the rest of the TUC proposals.

The talks therefore continued for one more day, until 2 November. At the last session, the Prime Minister took the lead, delivering a long statement.[101] The end of the talks was at hand and the fissure was laid open, with posturing by both sides seeking to avoid suffering blame for the failure.[102] The Prime Minister in effect delivered an "off-limits" to the TUC on the "other issues" raised in the General Council's statement. Just as Robert Carr had told the

TUC in October 1970, when he discussed the Consultative Document on the industrial relations policies, there could be discussions about details of certain matters, but the policies were Government responsibility and were not negotiable. In this case, these policies included membership of the European Community, the Housing Finance Act, and the Industrial Relations Act. Then, the Prime Minister went on to reiterate his 26 September proposals and to sweeten them by adding four new proposals dealing with pensions, needs allowance, family income supplement and other social matters. In the end, though, the TUC complained that the Prime Minister had not really made any new concessions. Moreover, the TUC representatives charged that by placing "off limits" markers everywhere, the Prime Minister was in effect withdrawing his offer of tripartite management of the economy.

The talks thus ended in failure. To no one's surprise, the Prime Minister announced a statutory standstill on pay and prices four days later. TUC negotiators and their colleagues on the General Council were quite relieved that the pressure was off. But the TUC withdrew to Congress House harbouring considerable frustration. Its leaders had decided to refuse agreement in order to preserve unity, but they had taken this action at the expense of genuine policy goals which these same leaders believed would be helpful to the interests of its member unions.

For its part, the Government also suffered from the failure of the talks.[103] Heath was bitterly disappointed. He had staked his own reputation on his U-turn toward collectivism. Moreover, he recognized that there would be need to develop further stages of incomes restraint whose success would still depend ultimately on the cooperation of obviously intransigent unionists. But there could be no turning back toward confrontation; that approach had failed completely. His and his Government's dilemma therefore removed the question of how they could induce cooperation.

F. RENEWED CONFLICT AND RENEWED COLLECTIVISM, 1973

Given their own substantive policy goals, it was hardly surprising that the TUC and the Government resumed sparring over the question of further dialogue and possible cooperation from almost the moment that the talks collapsed. There was the inevitable period of recrimination about who was to blame for the failure of the Chequers and Downing Street sessions. At the beginning of 1973, however, attention moved away from retrospective squabbling to the prospective question of Stage II of the pay and prices legislation. Both sides sought each other out: the Government to consult about their plans for the next stage, the TUC generally to protest against the operation of the standstill, especially the "inequity" of limited price control while wages remained completely frozen.[104] The TUC repeatedly dangled the possibility of renewed talks before the Government, but its demands remained the same as before plus insisting that the Government agree to a collective bargaining. Since the Government refused any immediate return to free bargaining – promising only that Stage III would be more relaxed – the TUC announced in mid-January that it would not cooperate in the second phase. When the Government then announced its plans for Stage II, the General Council added that it would not participate in the two new agencies set up to monitor the continued restraint – the Pay Board and the Price Commission.[105]

Stage II limited the size of pay increases for a work group to £1 plus 4 per cent of the current pay bill excluding overtime.[106] Negotiators were free to decide how to divide settlements but no individual could receive an increase of more than £250 per annum. On prices, most manufactured goods and services were controlled to the extent that manufacturers were limited to increases that met unavoidable costs or where products were being sold at a loss or investment inhibited. But prices of fresh food, seasonal food, imports, exports and items whose prices are affected primarily by international prices remained uncontrolled.

The TUC was little pleased by limited collective bargaining, and their leaders were particularly unhappy by the Government's additional caution that statutory incomes policy would be needed in some form for years to come. The evidence was now accumulating of how damaging the price–wage ratio was in practice. Prices of food, in particular, were rising at an unprecedented pace of more than twice as fast as for all other prices.[107] Housing costs, especially in London, were skyrocketing. Thus, while wage controls imposed a ceiling of about 6–7 per cent on effective wage increases, there seemed to be no limit to price rises. Worse still, the floating pound had by then been devalued by an effective rate of 10 per cent at just the time when the prices of commodities on the world market, also uncontrolled in British markets, were rising by more than 20 per cent annually.

It seemed at Congress House during that winter that Government policy had become inflexible again, though Heath and his colleagues were still urging cooperation. The Government was still anxious to hold discussions with the TUC, but union arguments seemed to have no effect on policy decisions. In frustration, Congress House began to listen more seriously to shop steward demands for renewed conflict and especially for resistance against further negotiations.

The General Council in part reflected this pressure in its February decision to call a Special Congress for March to discuss the economic situation.[108] It was the third Special Congress to be called within a four-year period but only the fourth one in half a century. The two previous Congresses met during extreme crises: the first to deal with the *In Place of Strife* negotiations and the second, in 1971, to plan public confrontation with the Government over the Industrial Relations Act. The Special Congress in 1973 met during a period marred less by crisis than by growing tension and worry that government policies foretold the beginning of a new wave of danger for the movement.

The General Council's main purpose in calling the Special Congress was to organize and rally opposition to the Government's announcement of a possibly permanent incomes policy. While the TUC expected progressive stages of restraint, Congress House was surprised by the announcement that the policy would last for at least three years, with the possibility of a two-year extension. This news, coupled with the extraordinary rise in prices of seasonal food, was especially troubling.[109] But the main fear was permanent incomes policy. TUC leaders believed that Government was attempting to resolve the dilemma posed by the Chequers and Downing Street stalemate by working in a direction opposite to Heath's proposals: that is, not toward but away from future union participation or influence in economic decision-making.[110] Thus, it seemed for a time that winter that having failed in its Industrial Relations Act and its *de facto* incomes policy in the public sector, the Government was about to shift gears again and use the failure of the talks as an excuse to stage a new attack on union power.

The Special Congress demonstrated that union executives and shop stewards away from the centre were willing both to vocalize their opposition to the Government's policy in consonance with General Council proposals, as well as to go beyond the Council views to support tangible industrial action.[111] Militant leaders at the Congress, for example, won delegate support at the outset by "referring back" the General Council report.[112] The General Council then hurriedly went into session as the Congress stood in recess and returned with a recommendation for a one-day national strike – something which it had resisted on a number of previous occasions. A rival motion asked the delegates to go further. At the end of the day, the Congress accepted the resolution providing for the one-day strike and only narrowly defeated the motion for a policy of continuing industrial action by the TUC against the Government's "counter-inflation laws".[113]

The Congress, at the same time, vividly demonstrated its sense of real policy frustration. Frank Chapple, General Secretary of the Electrical, Electronic, Telecommunication and Plumbing Trades Union, summed up much of the feeling:

> Most of the speeches that we have heard so far have indicated the horns of the dilemma upon which the Movement finds itself caught. On the one hand, if we give some assistance to the Government in order to help to get inflation under control, we may be guilty of also getting them re-elected whilst, on the other hand, if we do not give them any help and judging from the speeches so far heard, we are not likely to – the situation will become worse, inflation will get worse and thus our lot would be worse.[114]

Chapple spoke as an important right-wing figure on the General Council but the dilemma was well understood by the majority of his colleagues at that moment. Speaker after speaker pointed with exasperation to the rise in housing costs of more than 45 per cent in a year and the rise in food costs of more than 25 per cent during the same period.[115] The threat of continuous restraints on income therefore from a Government which did not then look likely to be soon turned out of office was a bitter prospect. Their "victories" over the Industrial Relations Act and in other confrontations with the Government had produced little gain for their substantive interests. The one-day strike was to be more an angry outburst than the confident act of a self-consciously powerful movement.

The TUC thus emerged from the Special Congress in both a mood of belligerence and of frustration tinged with a sense of impotence. The General Council would lead the one-day national strike while a majority were also anxious to find some route to renewed policy leverage. During April the General Council operated in both directions. It planned the 1 May strike at the same time as its members met secretly on an individual basis with the Prime Minister, listening to his urgings for renewed discussions about Stage II, which Heath predicted would come into effect during the late fall.[116]

These "talks about talks"[117] entered a more intensive phase once the 1 May demonstrations were over.[118] The Government showed growing impatience to begin new formal discussions. The Prime Minister held not only private chats with union leaders but tried to entice their interest by making policy shifts which would provide them with an argument that would convince their constituent members that new talks with the Government might be worth while.

One important example of change was the Prime Minister's statements indicating his new flexibility on the future of the Act. As early as 29 March, Heath publicly extended an invitation to the TUC to discuss the principles and the details of the working of the Act. He repeated this offer several times over the following weeks, both in private and in public. Just as important though, was his Government's new concern about food prices during that same period.

The constant barrage of TUC criticism about soaring food prices seemed to have finally hit its mark in early April as the Minister for Agriculture, Joseph Godber, responded with surprising virulence to EEC proposals for new Common Agricultural Price rises during 1973.[119] Godber not only promised to resist those rises but said he would demand an intensive review of the whole CAP as part of an effort to protect Britain from what he thought were unfair and unwarranted rises. Later that month when he returned from a Luxembourg meeting of Agriculture Ministers carrying promises of concessions on price increase and a review of the CAP in the fall of 1973, the Prime Minister could point to tangible Government movement toward TUC views.

The TUC viewed the Prime Minister's initiatives during the spring as very encouraging. TUC leaders believed that though the Government had become genuinely worried about food prices during the winter and early spring, the Government's move was primarily caused by union pressure which the TUC had kept up on almost a daily basis since the period of the Chequers and Downing Street talks.[120] It was from this positive analysis that the General

Council during May finally accepted Heath's invitation to have new talks about the economy. They accepted Godber's "triumph" in Luxembourg as evidence that there might be new value in talking with Heath. Some members of the General Council went so far as to believe that the Prime Minister had indeed met their "informal" price for talks.

Members of the TUC Economic Committee went even further in assessing the situation; the recent price rises, they believed, had weakened the Government position appreciably. The TUC could therefore undertake the talks from greater relative strength compared to the TUC position during Chequers and Downing Street.[121] TUC strategy from the outset was therefore to stress the same demands it had failed to win during the long round of talks: prices, the non-operation of the Industrial Relations Act, housing, and the post-freeze goal of a return as soon as possible to free collective bargaining.[122] It would discuss these questions as long as the Government wanted and there seemed any chance of success. But it entered the new talks little inclined to give much ground. As earlier, the TUC price for agreement was very high, probably higher even than before. The General Council again, it must be stressed, did not believe that the Prime Minister would be prepared to go that far.

The formal talks opened in July to few illusions about agreement. The media from the earliest were more perceptive this time in pointing out that the TUC was holding firm to nearly the same demands that it had failed to win during the Chequers and Downing Street talks eight months earlier.[123] The talks dragged on from the summer into the fall. For a variety of reasons, none of the participants wanted to break off relations again. The unions wanted to avoid the "spoiler" role and hoped anyway that the Government might eventually come around to the union position.[124] The CBI hoped against hope that the talks would succeed because the CBI worried that Stage III might produce an intolerable price squeeze against its member firms.[125] The Government, for its part, continued to want collectivist cooperation if possible, and if not, hoped to win at least informal union acquiesence for Stage III.

Many Tory backbenchers and even some Cabinet members, by contrast, strongly opposed the talks from the beginning.[126] They believed that the Chequers and Downing Street failure provided ample evidence that the trade union movement could not and would not commit itself to cooperation on wage restraint at any price. Moreover, they distrusted the TUC's partisan motives. They could not ignore the union movement's special quarrel with Conservatives, which proceeded from traditional hostility enhanced by the bitter struggle with this Government. So the Heath initiative looked both useless and dangerous.

The Prime Minister operated from a different perspective. The Chequers and Downing Street talks had been a serious disappointment but he remained more impressed by the failure of two years of all-out confrontation that had preceded the talks.[127] Much as Victor Feather did, Heath looked back on that period as tragically sterile. Though Heath was well known to be feisty and unintimidated by union power, he preferred rational dialogue with rational men leading to agreeable and sensible solutions. The two years' struggle had not produced sensible policies and he now resented the advice of fellow Tories who argued that the lesson of the first two years' conflict with unions was that he should lead an even stouter fight.[128] These same advisers had constructed the Industrial Relations Act and Heath now believed that the Act demonstrated the danger of inflexible structures which ignored the collectivist strain in the British polity. In essence, trade union leaders like Victor Feather had made their point with the Prime Minister in arguing that he could not simply turn his back or legislate an end to collectivist politics.

The irony of the Prime Minister's collectivist commitment in mid-1973 was that he found support for this position primarily from his non-political advisers rather than from his political colleagues. The *Sunday Times* Insight team in its study '*The Fall of Edward Heath*' identified this team of civil servants who bolstered Heath at this time.[129] The leading figure was Sir William Armstrong, the powerful head of the Civil Service who became responsible for incomes policy. The group also included "Douglas Allen (Head of the Treasury), Robert Armstrong (Heath's principal private secretary), [and] Burke Trend (Cabinet Secretary)".[130]

Armstrong, in particular, was the major figure who bolstered the Prime Minister and helped crystallize his collectivist purpose in 1972 and 1973. Like Heath, Armstrong was a strong, confident figure who believed deeply in rationality. Though he had little experience with trade union leaders, Armstrong believed that rational discussion and negotiation could produce workable policy.

Both Armstrong and Heath remained firmly committed to this

view throughout the second round of talks during 1973. But the
most crucial test lay ahead. The climactic encounter between
government and the union movement proved to be the second
dispute with the miners' union, which occurred during the fall and
winter of 1973–74. Rail and electrical workers also staged pay
disputes during this same period, but it was the miners who wielded
the dramatic power.

The Yom Kippur War in October pushed the economy into a
considerably more vulnerable position. Energy stocks shrunk
quickly in reaction to the Arab oil boycott and the miners could
thereby gain enormous leverage by their ban on overtime work
which union leaders imposed in mid-November. Within a few
weeks, the Government sombrely warned that the country stood at
the brink of economic disaster. It was in meeting this crisis that
Heath's strategy failed completely.

G. THE CATASTROPHE OF THE MINERS' DISPUTE

The difficulty with Edward Heath's brand of collectivist politics was
that he substituted rationality for politics. At nearly every point in
dealing with the miners' dispute, the Prime Minister – ironically the
leading politician in Britain – failed to understand and deal perceptively with the political choices he faced. In part, Heath suffered
from his excessive dedication to rationalism and his own personality
which excluded the kind of interaction which trade unionists expect
to have with adversaries whether in political or industrial bargaining. But in another part, Heath suffered from the traditional
problems that his Tory detractors had claimed make it difficult for
Conservatives to deal with trade unionists. These problems included class differences and the long history of cool and distant
relations, both of which were enhanced by the irritating policies
administered by his own administration. The sum of these necessarily intruded whatever the good intentions he showed by his
attitudinal U-turn.

A secret meeting between the Prime Minister and the miners'
union President, Joe Gormley, on 16 July 1973 marked the
beginning of the series of fateful political mistakes that led the
Government into its disastrous election of February 1974.[131] The
Prime Minister had initiated the meeting with Gormley in
conjunction with the opening of talks with the TUC because he
feared that the miners would provide the most dangerous threat to

his Stage III plans. The miners' strike in 1972 had been one of the key benchmarks in Heath's conversion to collectivism. By that strike, the miners had destroyed his *de facto* wage policy in the public sector, seriously impairing his broader economic policy and demonstrating that such conflict was both dangerous and futile. It was not hard for Heath to remember his own words at the end of that earlier strike, which were that some better way had to be found to settle such disputes.[132]

The Prime Minister invited the miners' union President to Downing Street against a background of reports that the miners were preparing to plan a new very large pay claim. Gormley and Heath did not know each other very well, since Gormley was not part of the TUC inner circle who met regularly with the Government. But Heath's advisers did view Gormley as a powerful leader who had courageously won his position a couple of years earlier running in the union election against the flamboyant Communist, Mick McGahey, who still served as the miners' Vice-President. Moreover, Gormley seemed to have been quite influential during the strike and its settlement in early 1972.

The Prime Minister therefore thought that he was taking a sensible political initiative.[133] The talks that day led to what both men believed was a deal which would avoid a miners' strike during the following winter. Gormley believed that the Prime Minister was prepared to "wink" at his own Stage III.[134] The miners, he understood, would be recognized as a special case entitled to extra compensation under a Stage III provision allowing for payment for "unsocial hours". Heath thought that Gormley had promised to win his executive's acceptance of a new contract based on the provision for extra compensation.

The deal from the Prime Minister's perspective was an admirable trade-off; he thought it was sealed and all but delivered from the time it was agreed.[135] The disaster of its implementation proved, however, that the Government completely misread or did not read at all the politics of the miners' union. The Prime Minister sensibly recognized potential trouble from the miners but he operated from a very limited understanding of the miners' demands, their intensity, or the position of its leadership. Joe Gormley was never as well placed to dictate to his executive as Heath and his advisers assumed. Moreover, inflation during the previous two years had stirred rising rank-and-file anger at the decline of their wages compared to other industries, with the gap even wider than during the strike of 1972.[136] Therefore the problem, that of implementing the Gormley–Heath plan, went far beyond simply shaking hands at Downing Street. If Heath wanted Gormley to succeed, he needed to give him powerful but indirect help. But the Prime Minister, by contrast, offered no help.

The Coal Board made its new contract offer at nearly the same moment in October that the Government published its consultative document on Stage III.[137] The Government kept its bargain with Gormley in strict terms: Stage III would contain a provision allowing for extra compensation to workers who laboured "unsocial hours".[138] The Coal Board took up this passage in offering a package increase of somewhat more than 16 per cent. The increase would include the 7 per cent provided for under Stage III for all workers; the possibility of more than 3 per cent in productivity increases; about 1.5 per cent miscellaneous increases plus the 4.5 per cent in "unsocial hours" increase.

Heath expected that Gormley would take the offer to his Executive Committee and after hearing a few grumbles, win its approval in fairly short order. Heath was fully aware of militant demands for much higher rises but he assumed that the Coal Board's offer was so generous that it would stand, with a little help from Gormley, on its own merits.

The Prime Minister's expectations were quickly shattered as the Executive Committee turned the offer down. However generous the offer, it did not begin to satisfy militants who had been promising a full fight all during the summer and into the fall. Furthermore, the Coal Board had fed militant expectations by unstrategically making their maximum offer right at the beginning. There was no room for bargaining and thus Gormley and other moderates had no leverage to use against the militant argument.[139] Trade unionists inevitably expect to do better than the first offer in any negotiations, a rule which was especially applicable in the charged atmosphere of miners' politics that autumn.

At bottom, though, the Prime Minister suffered from misunderstanding Gormley's position within the union. Though President, Gormley had never commanded the kind of loyalty or influence that Heath knew that other prominent TUC leaders held. Rather, Gormley suffered a militant-dominated executive who could not early decide to come to terms with this Government. Not only did the miners remember their 1972 success and their relative wage slippage since that time, but they viewed the Government with more hostility than did most of the trade union movement. Heath was at a disadvantage in learning these insights about the miners. TUC leaders themselves were not close to the miners and therefore could not offer cogent advice – if, which is doubtful, they were willing to be so forthcoming during the critical period leading up to the Coal Board's offer.

The failure by Heath and his Government to deal astutely with the miners seemed to confirm the wisdom that Conservative leaders had repeated over the years – at least since the 1926 General Strike – that the miners were one union with which a Tory Government should not tangle. Heath apparently learned that lesson in 1972, but by late 1973 he took a feisty view of the miners' rejection of the Coal Board offer, seeing it as a political challenge rather than an economic response. By late November, the Prime Minister had reached the conclusion that the miners had refused the offer in favour of adopting the political goal of bringing down his Government and perhaps the entire political system.[140] It was based on this miscalculation, added to earlier ones, that Prime Minister Heath proceeded during the next two months toward disaster.

The Government's strategy and tactics were almost entirely in the hands of Prime Minister Heath from early December onward.[141] He brought one of his most trusted political colleagues, William Whitelaw, into the dispute. Whitelaw had made a considerable name for himself in dealing with Northern Ireland. His reputation was that of a patient, conciliatory politician with considerable negotiating skill. Heath's appointment of him to be Minister for Employment to replace Maurice Macmillan therefore seemed to signal the Prime Minister's faith that Whitelaw could bring his mediating talents into the crisis. But it was soon apparent that Heath had failed to give Whitelaw authority to negotiate terms any different from those that the Coal Board had offered and the miners had rejected in the first place.

Whitelaw's presence, however, raised considerable optimism that Heath was about to make a new initiative. At first, the miners' executive shared this optimism. Shortly after his appointment, Whitelaw met with Gormley (again in secret) to find out the miners' terms for settlement.[142] Later, on 20 December, Whitelaw met with the entire executive and several NUM participants gained the impression that he was searching for areas in Stage III which might be used by the Pay Board to allow for a larger pay increase.[143] For example, the discussion focused on the possibility of paying miners for washing-up time and for the time they wait to be taken to the coal-face. But later, when the Coal Board asked Whitelaw whether it should take up this ploy, Whitelaw replied that the Board should not use devious exceptions.[144]

The miners' bitterness at what they thought was deception by the Government added to the intractibility of the dispute. The NUM executive came to believe during this period that the Government was working to avoid a settlement. For many of them, the dispute during December took on the sort of political overtones which Heath had earlier attributed to their motives.

The Prime Minister, from the NUM perspective, was now showing evidence that he was working up a crisis atmosphere directed toward a snap election which would challenge not only the claim of the miners but the power of the trade union movement – in much the same way that he had challenged the trade union movement over the first two years of his Government. Besides the Whitelaw deception, the miners subsequently took as evidence Heath's inclusion of emergency measures which greatly charged the crisis atmosphere.

The TUC Steps In

It was the Prime Minister's 13 December speech announcing the three-day week to begin from 30 December that brought the TUC actively into the dispute. Before that moment, Congress House and Whitehall had only fleeting, inconsequential contacts about the problem. Worried TUC leaders had watched from a distance as the two sides hardened their positions and began to politicize their perceptions of each other's motives. The Government seemed to be retreating into the hostile, mistrusting attitude of two years earlier. As each day went by, the miners moved closer to the sort of political opposition which the Prime Minister seemed to think they held at just the previous moment. The process was a self-fulfilling prophecy, and now, with the three-day week staring them in the face, TUC leaders became anxious to head off what they feared would be a disaster.[145]

The irony haunting the TUC as it moved aggressively into the dispute was that the "success" of its resistance to Heath's initiatives toward cooperation during the previous eighteen months made it difficult for them now to demand the Government's ear at this moment of crisis. Though the Prime Minister had pressed for collectivist management of the economy since July 1972, no means of participation was now available. The TUC had refused the place that the Prime Minister offered. In addition, the long fruitless months of talking had added to the Prime Minister's distrust of union leaders and their motives. While Heath viewed the miners as a self-consciously independent group and understood that the major trade union leaders themselves did not know their brethren at the NUM very well, he had no trouble in believing that the TUC at least enjoyed the miners' role as a political "stalking horse" for the Labour party.[146]

Whatever may have been the Prime Minister's perceptions of TUC motives for entering the dispute, the members of the General Council and their new General Secretary, Len Murray, were clear about their purposes. They urgently wanted the Government to end the three-day week because it posed the gravest threat to the livelihood of every trade unionist in Britain.[147] They also wanted to dissuade the Chancellor from implementing the particularly savage cuts in public spending which he announced on 13 December. But at the same time they worried that they were losing leverage with the Prime Minister as it seemed he now had more to gain from staging a snap election than from further talking. In sum, the TUC pressed hard during these weeks for an end to the miners' dispute and the three-day week.[148]

TUC negotiators in several meetings with Ministers and the Prime Minister repeated these purposes constantly in late December and early January.[149] They pointed out, for example, during a special meeting of the National Economic Development Council on 21 December that not only would the three-day work week be counter-productive but that if the Government was trying "to put pressure on certain groups of workers [by the three-day week] then this would only have the effect of hardening attitudes."[150] They urged the Government to change its stance in dealing with the miners, to recognize the special problems of the miners, and to use provisions of its own legislation to grant them extra compensation.

Nothing budged the Government's position. On 9 January, the TUC in desperation, went much further at a meeting at the NEDC. It offered the Government an arrangement which it felt would provide the rationale for a settlement.[151] The TUC promised that "if the Government were prepared to give an assurance that it would make possible a settlement between the miners and the National Coal Board, other unions would not use this as an argument in negotiations for their own settlements".[152] As the *Sunday Times* reported, the offer took the Government and the CBI representatives by such surprise that Sir Sidney Greene, who delivered the proposal to the head of the TUC economics committee "felt obliged to repeat it".[153]

TUC representatives had decided to take this initiative earlier that day in an effort to meet the Government's most often stated concern that any concession to the miners in this case would be used by trade unionists everywhere to breach Stage III.[154] They felt they were making a bold move in a dangerous situation. The offer was sincere.[155] But the Chancellor's immediate reaction at the NEDC meeting that afternoon was to reject the offer by arguing that the miners had already gained special treatment by the terms of the original offer. Barber added that he thought giving additional considerations would be unfair to those workers who had already settled under Stage III, and at any rate he doubted whether the TUC could ensure that other unions would not take advantage of the miners' gains.

The TUC Economic Committee met the next day and again on 14 January with the Prime Minister to press their offer further.[156] But the Prime Minister's reaction was negative. TUC representatives vigorously pressed Heath to reverse his position, adding that they were prepared to win the backing of union executives for their commitment at a Special Conference on 16 January. To this, the Prime Minister wondered especially about how much of an absolute guarantee union leaders could provide. He repeated the same argument that afternoon in answering questions about the offer in the House of Commons.[157]

The question of "copper-bottomed guarantees" then reared its head again. During *In Place of Strife*, it was the Labour Government that wanted "copper-bottomed guarantees"; then the TUC during the Chequers and Downing Street talks; and now the Tory Government looked sceptically at a TUC offer and wanted some proof, some solid evidence that the TUC would keep its word. This time the Government suffered paranoia about political conspiracy. Whereas only a few months earlier, the Prime Minister was willing gladly to settle for TUC "assurances" of a voluntary wages policy, now he wanted guarantees. Yet, ironically, both his Government and the TUC had a solid stake in a peaceful settlement. Though many Tories wanted to have it out with the unions, to force their argument in an election, the Prime Minister himself wanted to solve the dispute peacefully.[158] But there could be no backing down: the miners, he believed, had been given a generous offer. The fact that they did not settle on this "rational" basis demonstrated that their motives in the conflict were political.[159]

The Prime Minister and many of his Cabinet believed the TUC's motives were equally suspect. Heath distrusted the 9 January offer; why, he asked, "had the TUC sprung the offer on the Government without prior discussion?"[160] The aggression displayed by Labour MPs about the offer that afternoon in the House of Commons question time demonstrated, as far as Heath was concerned, that the TUC was pulling a public relations stunt rather than making a serious offer.[161] Furthermore, Heath very much distrusted the behaviour of Len Murray, whom he viewed as a cynical partisan given to devious conspiracy. He missed very much the contact with Victor Feather, who had now retired.[162] It was Feather who acted as the catalyst during 1972 and 1973 for bringing the Government and TUC back into contact. Heath had admired Feather as a reasonable man whose word could be trusted; Murray was still mostly an unknown but Heath strongly disliked his first contacts with the new General Secretary.

It was in this poisonous atmosphere that the Government continued to reject the TUC offer, completely missing the opportunity for settling the dispute. The terms provided in effect for the counter-inflation policy that Heath himself had sought in bargaining sessions over many months. The TUC wanted and needed to restore its members to full-time work; it was willing to pay the price necessary to win a settlement. The Prime Minister turned his back in anger.

The chance for reaching a settlement declined precipitously in the days after the 14 January meeting. The Special Conference of TUC Union Chief Officers on 16 January overwhelmingly endorsed the TUC initiative and the position the General Council had taken in reacting to the Government's emergency policies.[163] But the Conference did little to influence the Government's position, which Heath reconfirmed again at the last meeting, which dismissed the offer on 21 January.[164] At that session, the TUC pressed its offer again and again. Heath's answer each time showed that he was still worried about the precedent of breaking the Stage III guidelines and as the TUC charged, also worried about "public reactions to a departure from what had previously been its rigid attitude".[165] The *Sunday Times* adds that "The occasion is remembered mainly for its long silences. Heath sat for minutes on end, head sunk deep on chest, pondering gloomily but saying nothing. To one witness, he seemed to *want* to say something, but could not manage to. With desperate urgency, Hugh Scanlon addressed one ultimate question to him. 'Is there anything, anything at all, that we can do or say which will satisfy you?' The question went unanswered."[166]

The last chance for settlement developed a few days later with the publication of the Pay Board's long-awaited report on pay relativities.[167] The report offered a real basis for settlement because it proposed a mechanism for providing increases outside an incomes policy such as Stage III. The report recommended establishment of a Relativities Board that would hear the complaints of working groups which believed that they were underpaid as compared to other groups. The Relativities Board would be able to designate that a working group was special in some way and could thus be given special pay consideration. The opportunity was obvious, but the Prime Minister and his Employment Secretary missed their chance again.

The Government blundered in viewing the relativities mechanism as applicable only to conditions of normal work, not to industrial disputes. Thus, the Prime Minister mistakenly proposed in a letter to TUC leaders that they meet with him to discuss how the Relativities report could be applied to the miners' situation *after settlement*.[168] He offered, for example, the possibility that, if the miners would resume normal work and accept a settlement within Stage III, they could then make their case ". . . for a relative improvement in their position to be examined in accordance with the procedure described in the Relativities report when it is brought into operation".[169]

Since the purpose of the Prime Minister's suggestion was also to influence the miners toward settlement, criticism of the Government's judgement seems especially justified. The letter was sent to the TUC on 30 January, at the same moment that the miners' rank and file were voting on their Executive's recommendation for a national strike. It was therefore made too late to affect the vote. Moreover, even if the proposal might have helped, it did not provide the immediate pay offer that the miners had been seeking. In a letter to the Leader of the Opposition, Harold Wilson, Heath stressed that the Relativities report did not suggest that the miners' claim should be "urgently examined as an exceptional case".[170] The Government therefore gave the impression to the TUC that it was using the Relativities report as part of a propaganda campaign in preparation for an election.[171] Heath lent credence to this view just the night before he sent his letter to the TUC, by his comments about the remarks of Michael McGahey, the Communist Vice-President of the NUM. McGahey had said that he would appeal for help from the troops if they were called in to move coal during a miners' strike.[172] In answer, Mr Heath charged that some of the miners' executives, like Mr McGahey, regarded the dispute as a political matter. They were not interested, Heath said, in settling a wage dispute. They were interested in " . . . smashing what is accepted as fair now by five million people [Stage III] and to get rid of the elected government of the day".[173]

More than 80 per cent of the miners who voted by secret ballot supported their executive's recommendation to strike. Thus, by the time the TUC met with the Prime Minister on 4 February to discuss his proposals for setting up the Relativities Board, the situation was in full crisis. The meeting has been described by one of those present as doomed to fail in advance because by then an immediate election seemed certain.[174] Nevertheless, the TUC team did make one final effort to convince the Government to take a more flexible position. They argued with the Prime Minister that he needed to deal squarely with the problem of the miners' immediate demand for "cash on the table"; he should not delude himself into thinking that the Relativities report could be helpful in heading off a strike at this point. They added that if the Government would authorize the Coal Board to start talks with the miners as a special case, the TUC itself would attempt to convince the NUM to postpone its strike. But the Prime Minister would have none of it and the talks ended in complete failure. Three days later, on 7 February, Edward Heath announced to no one's surprise that there would be an election.

The miners' strike and attendant economic crisis dominated the campaign. The Government began as the clear favourite to retain office but proved to be its own worst enemy. Only one day after the Prime Minister announced the dissolution of Parliament and set the election for 28 February, Whitelaw asked the Pay Board to study the question of relativities as it would apply to the miners' claim. The widespread impression was that the Employment Secretary could well have taken the same action much earlier.[175] His initiative thereby seriously undermined the rationale which most people believed the Prime Minister had used for calling the election.

The Pay Board study reappeared to haunt the Government again on 21 February. At the Board's hearings, Derek Robinson, the deputy chairman of the Pay Board, offered statistics which showed that the Government had based the Coal Board's offer on incorrect calculations.[176] Robinson insisted that the offer should have been higher. Though the Prime Minister vigorously denied any mistake, Harold Wilson immediately seized the issue with delight. It proved to be the most crucial issue of the campaign because Labour effectively made the double-barrelled complaint that the Government had blundered in its arithmetic and thereby necessarily caused hardships not only for the miners and their families, but for everyone in the country who was suffering from the deprivation caused by the three-day week.

Labour steadily cut into the Conservative lead, though most of the polls still predicted that the Government would retain office. But on 28 February the voters gave the Labour Party a razor-thin victory, though lacking a majority of seats in the Commons. After a few days of hesitation, Heath resigned and Harold Wilson returned as Prime Minister of the first minority government of the post-World War II era.

Within a week after Labour took office, the Coal Board, with the new Government's blessing, used the newly-published Relativities report as the basis for settling with the miners. The new contract called for increases ranging from 22 to 32 per cent. The three-day work week ended at the same time.

H. CONCLUDING COMMENTS

This story of missed opportunities and policy frustrations is interesting by itself. Yet its importance lies in the legacies which the experience produces for union–Conservative Government relations in the future. The prospect is that the union movement will suffer from this relationship, and probably suffer more than will future Conservative Governments.

The Conservatives and their leader took considerable punishment from their union adversaries between 1970 and 1974. The miners' strike was a real tragedy for Edward Heath. He missed the crucial opportunities for settling the dispute. He could have come to terms with the TUC and saved his painfully constructed incomes policy. But he completely misunderstood the sincerity of the TUC's offer. He failed to appreciate the TUC's overriding interest in ending the three-day week rather than in putting him out of office.

At the same time, the course of the miners' dispute and in fact the whole period after Heath's conversion to collectivist politics in mid-1972 were also a bitter experience for the union movement. The General Council could not agree to accept the role its senior leaders would have wanted in jointly managing the economy. Though the members of the General Council could well envision the value of protecting their members' economic interests, the prospect of cooperating with the Tory "enemies" proved too divisive. Sabotaging the tripartite talks, whatever their merits, became the only alternative course of action. Later, the General Council would regret its lack of access and influence with the Prime Minister and his Cabinet. Faced with the miners' dispute, the TUC could not overcome the Prime Minister's mistrust and suspicion. The General Council worked frantically but ineffectively that winter of 1974, trying to get its members back to full-time work. But the Prime Minister would not accept the credibility of the TUC's offer to make the miners a special case.

Defeat was traumatic for the Conservative Party, but it was just as traumatic for the TUC. Though union wounds were salved by Labour's return to office, the spectacle of the TUC's impotence during the miners' dispute was not lost at Congress House. For the first time, the traditionally hostile and ugly relationship between the Conservative Party and the union movement worked against the unions – as well as the Party. Before, the TUC had enjoyed its vetoes of Conservative economic policy and had retired from interaction secure in the knowledge that the Tories would still defend the basic economic security provided by the 1944 economic and social contract. But all that had changed. The TUC learned that the deterioration in the appeal of Keynesian wisdom compelled them to defend their interests by winning influence and access to government policy-making. However, the General Council felt restrained by internal union politics which still dictated that the TUC must conflict with or at least refuse to cooperate with the Tories even at the price of diminished influence. The TUC General Council thus learned in 1973 and 1974 that Churchill's warning about the dangers of union–Conservative relations now also applied to them.

The problem that the TUC faces for the future is that it will probably suffer from the same dilemma – or worse – during the life of the next Tory Government. The General Council will certainly continue to have a vital stake in exercising influence on economic policy in an aggressive manner, but internal union pressure will make such a move difficult. At the same time, based on current statements, the next Tory Government will probably go out of its way to avoid entangling relations with the union movement. James Prior, the shadow Employment Minister, has said repeatedly that the next Conservative Government will not seek conflict with the union movement by legislating a new Industrial Relations Act. Mrs Thatcher has added importantly that her government also looks forward to administering a monetarist economic policy free of incomes policies and other sorts of entrapping relationships with the union movement. She promises to consult with the unions, but to deprive them of the instruments, such as incomes policies, which she believes they have used so skilfully to frustrate and paralyze the policies of earlier Tory Governments.

Congress House thus contemplates an unhappy dilemma. It must overcome the force of traditional relations with the Conservatives as they affect internal union politics, while also somehow overcoming the avowed Tory wish to avoid union influence altogether.

4 Recession, Social Contracts and the Labour Government of 1974

Labour's return to office in March 1974 was a welcome surprise for trade unionists. All through the miners' dispute General Council leaders worried that Heath would take advantage of the crisis in order to win a crushing election victory on the theme "Who runs Britain?". Not only did TUC leaders fear that a Tory victory would prolong the miners' strike and with it the three-day week, they also worried that the Government would resume its abandoned efforts to restrict union influence generally. The TUC had acted from these fears when the General Council offered to guarantee that a generous miners' settlement would not be used as a rationale for other union wage claims. Many union leaders had even regretted their decision to refuse the Prime Minister's several offers of tripartite influence and access which they might have used to good advantage during the miners' dispute.

Labour's upset victory was therefore especially pleasing. The miners' strike could be settled quickly and the country returned to full-time work. The prospect of renewed conflict with an electorally-strengthened Conservative Government was put to an end. And, perhaps even more importantly, the TUC would no longer suffer from so weak an influence on policy-making. Quite to the contrary, in fact, the TUC looked forward now to the incumbency of a Labour Government fully committed to serve the positive interests of trade unionism more than at any time since Attlee took office as Prime Minister in 1945.

These circumstances boded well for collectivist politics. Both TUC and Labour Party leaders in March 1974 started from a converging interest in developing cooperation while avoiding conflict between each other. The TUC held the upper hand at the beginning by virtue of its consecutive victories against two Governments which had attempted to alter and reduce its negative influence over economic policy-making. The Labour Party lived with the memories of *In Place of Strife* and the election defeat of 1970, both of which seemed to argue that Labour too should heed Churchill's prescriptive warning against making trouble with the unions – which he had meant only for Conservatives.

Balancing this union advantage, though, TUC leaders worried that they needed to cooperate with Labour while avoiding conflict in order to develop positive influence on economic policy-making. The fortuitous victory over the Heath Government could not hide the inability of the TUC to influence economic policy-making during the Heath years or moderate the Prime Minister's intransigent perceptions during the miners' dispute. Crisis or not, the General Council held a far more "realistic" view about economic management in 1974 than it had held in 1969. The Council was beginning to accept by then that it could only protect union interests by enjoying continued influential access to the economic decision-making and administration process. Its members believed that the TUC could no longer expect that governments of either party would follow some preconceived policy which would inevitably protect economic well-being.

Both of these balancing considerations worked during the life of the 1974 Labour Government. The TUC held the dominating leverage at the beginning. For a year and a half the Government loyally fulfilled its policy commitments and took the TUC into its closest confidence. Trade unionism thus enjoyed the fullest positive influence before recession, including very high inflation and unemployment, turned the advantage over to the political side of the Labour movement. By mid-1975 the Wilson Government could insist and win the first effective "voluntary" wage restraint in nearly three decades from a badly frightened union movement. With the British economy in severe crisis, the Labour Government for at least three years thereafter took its turn in producing effective collectivist politics by the strength of its control over economic management.

BUILDING THE SOCIAL CONTRACT

The development of converging and cooperative interests between the two sides of the Labour movement began in 1969 with the union movement holding the advantage in the wake of the settlement of

In Place of Strife. The Labour Government openly curried union favour in order to avoid further conflict during its remaining tenure. Then, in opposition, Harold Wilson worked to take advantage of the union–Heath conflict to further heal the battle-wounds. The TUC eagerly took up the healing process, going much further than developing the usual closer relations when Labour is in opposition. It sought to take advantage of union strength in order to cement substantive understanding with the Party about how the next Labour Government would behave. The TUC wanted to win agreements that both forestalled further conflict and provided guarantees that union interests would be promoted by favourable policies during the next Labour Government. Each battle with the Tory Government furthered this strategy, so that gradually the TUC won a comprehensive series of policy commitments.

The instrument for rebuilding the alliance between the two wings of the Labour movement was the Liaison Committee. First constituted in December 1970 in the midst of the debate over the Industrial Relations Bill,[1] the Liaison Committee included representatives from the General Council, the Labour Party's National Executive Committee and the Parliamentary Labour Party.

The Committee's structure and purpose recalled the National Joint Council which was constituted along much the same representational lines in 1932.[2] Like the Joint Council, the Liaison Committee began its work during a period of crisis in the wake of serious conflict between the unions and the Party. The Liaison Committee also worked during an era when Labour's weakness gave the TUC "a unique opportunity to press its views successfully on the party".[3] In that earlier time, the Joint Council had taken an ". . . active interest in economic policy and specifically initiated the collaboration between the TUC Economic Committee and the party's Research Department in the development of a common economic policy, especially economic reorganization. Also in 1933, the Joint Council was instrumental in influencing the party Conference, still reeling from the shock of 'MacDonaldism,' to accept a new set of rules intended to tie future Labour governments more closely to the wishes of the party organization and membership."[4]

The Liaison Committee developed less dramatic and far-reaching plans than the Joint Council but the degree of union influence was just as impressive. Harold Wilson's continued presence as leader of the Labour Party and prospective Prime

Minister encouraged the TUC to demand "copper-bottomed" policy agreements with their old adversary. Much as the spectre of MacDonald had haunted the work of the National Joint Council, Wilson's "treachery" stigmatized him as a "twister" who could not be fully trusted. Trade union leaders were willing to work with Wilson but he had completely exhausted his fund of trust and goodwill. Unionists insisted that they reach a clear understanding about what the next Labour Government would provide to induce their mutual cooperation.[5]

The course of relations between the TUC and the Heath Government generally dictated the pace, intensity and focus of the Liaison Committee's work. The Committee first met in December 1970 on an unofficial, informal basis. It met again twice during 1971. Those early meetings considered the strategy and details of Parliamentary action on the Industrial Relations Bill as well as the TUC's public campaign. Once the bill was assured of passage, the TUC pressed successfully in June 1971 for Party agreement that the next Labour Government would repeal the Act.

The Liaison Committee took on an official status, including regularly scheduled monthly meetings, at the beginning of 1972 as the Industrial Relations Act came into effect. The Committee set up work groups to examine a great number of issues including the future of industrial relations, the possibility of creating an independent conciliation and arbitration service, and the future of prices and incomes policy under the next Labour Government. These issues addressed controversies which were then current between the TUC and the Heath Government.

The Liaison Committee reached a peak in its work at the same time that the conflict over the Industrial Relations Act reached a crisis in July 1972. While the Pentonville dockers were destroying the Industrial Relations Act, the Liaison Committee issued its first major statement.[6] Point by point the Committee offered alternative Labour policies as contrast to the Government's troubles. Heath thereby unwittingly contributed to rapprochement between the two wings of the labour movement largely on terms which the unions dictated but could not win in dealing with his Government. Heath's own about-face toward collectivist politics that summer occurred in part because the Prime Minister worried that the renewed labour alliance would add to the prospect that the union movement would act more boldly and perhaps destructively.

The Liaison Committee's July 1972 statement set out the agreed details for policies that the next Labour Government would undertake. The first order of business would be the repeal of the Industrial Relations Act in the first session of the new Parliament. Then, the new Government would establish an independent Conciliation and Arbitration Service as proposed by the TUC. Together with a batch of other legislative actions, the Labour Government would thereby define a new pattern of peaceful but *voluntary* industrial relations.

The Liaison Committee at the same time announced that it would now proceed to define the next Labour Government's general economic policy, keeping in mind that it was not possible to know the conditions under which that Government would take office. But the Committee took as the basis for its economic considerations the primary importance of full employment and sustained economic expansion. It would recommend how best to promote these goals and therefore to deal with predictable obstacles such as the high rate of inflation, low investment and the chronic balance of payments problem.

Work continued apace as the TUC met with the Government in the Chequers and Downing Street talks during the fall of 1972. There was strain in the Liaison Committee at times when the union–Government negotiations seemed, at least publicly, to be heading toward some sort of agreement. But eventual consensus by the General Council against agreement with the Government enhanced the Committee's work and the tone of interpersonal relations. The price and wage freeze together with sudden price inflation during the winter and spring of 1973 encouraged the TUC defensively to press harder for the Committee to develop already-promised general economic prescriptions. Congress House took an aggressive lead at this time in offering substantive proposals.

The work of the Liaison Committee during the winter of 1973 offers an excellent commentary on union influence at that time. In February 1973 the Committee published its statement, *Economic Policy and the Cost of Living*.[7] Its proposals were almost precisely the same as the TUC unsuccessfully offered during the tripartite talks. Though obviously unacceptable to the Government and strategically useful to the TUC as one more rationale for sabotaging the talks, the proposals did represent a set of real union policy goals. To that extent the unions suffered important policy frustration when the talks failed in November. The subsequent freeze on wages and prices only added to this frustration because the freeze worked far more successfully against wage rises than against price rises, especially food and housing costs.[8] Therefore, the unions turned to the Liaison Committee to provide support for the policy goals which they had not won in bargaining with the Government.

This February statement did much to encourage development of what came to be known as the "social contract". The original idea for a social contract was born from the suggestion by Heath during the tripartite talks that unions, employers and Government become partners in a social contract to manage the economy. The concept was broad and involved trade-offs. When the unions rejected agreement, they took the concept of social contract with them to the Liaison Committee, where they processed the idea in a friendlier atmosphere, away from the pressures of immediate policy decision-making. The terms of the February statement offer the outlines of the social contract as it was to develop over the following months.

The key concept in that statement was that the problem of inflation could only be properly considered "within the context of a coherent economic and social strategy".[9] That strategy should give emphasis to overcoming the problems impeding Britain's economic growth and simultaneously promote cooperation between trade unions and government. The statement thus refuted, in TUC terms, the notion that inflation was due primarily to union wage demands. It also stressed the familiar union theme that remedies should include broad-gauged expansion, with government acting vigorously to restrain prices.

Food, housing and rents should be controlled as part of "a wide-ranging and permanent system of price controls", the report urged.[10] "Such a system will need, first, to cover the main items in the family budget and affect the various levels of activity, from manufacturing to retailing."[11] "There must be a new approach to housing and rents. The next Labour Government will repeal the 1972 Housing Finance Act. Council tenants will be given a better deal—both on rents and on security—and be given, too, very much more say in the management of their estates. But underpinning all of these policies, . . . must be agreed policies on investment, employment and economic growth. And the objective must be faster growth in both national output and in output per man. . . . And all of this will be backed by a policy of planned growth—allowing the economy to expand fast enough to keep unemployment down to a minimum level required for job changing and retraining."[12]

Four months later, during the early summer of 1973, the Liaison

Committee published another statement of agreement.[13] It announced that the Committee was proceeding to draft actual industrial relations legislation including three separate bills. First the next Labour Government would introduce a repeal bill which would both repeal the Industrial Relations Act and provide new protections for unions including improved provisions dealing with unfair dismissals. Then, the Government would proceed to legislate an Employment Protection Bill which would extend the rights of workers and unions including new protections for dismissals, redundancy, contracts of employment, etc. The last piece of legislation would be a "Companies Bill" and would provide for extending industrial democracy.

The details of the social contract were thus well in place before the miners' crisis of late 1973 and early 1974. Though the TUC did look forward hopefully to the next Labour Government, it made an all-out effort during the winter to help solve the miners' crisis without forcing a snap election. Leaders on the General Council genuinely worried that Prime Minister Heath would easily win such an election and that then the TUC would be saddled with an even more intransigent government.

Congress House was obviously delighted when Labour won the dreaded election. The General Council was even more pleased when the new Government proceeded with great speed to implement the terms of its agreements with the unions.[14] The fidelity of its work that spring was only matched by the fidelity of the Attlee Government to the much more thorough-going reforms and programme of public ownership which the Party and the TUC had agreed during the previous decade. The lessons of that earlier time were not forgotten, and the new Wilson Government worked to give substance to the very close relationship that had developed within the Liaison Committee while in Opposition.

The minority position of the new Government added pressure for carrying out the social contract. Wilson immediately directed his effort to a second election, much as he had in 1964. Again, as at that time, the quality of ties with the union movement was important and he accepted that the development of that relationship would strongly affect the possibility of producing a majority at the next polling. He not only needed traditional union votes, his Government had taken office at a time of high conflict with the union movement and Labour had to be seen as capable of producing cooperative economic management. If the social contract worked,

Wilson would be able to go to the country arguing that Labour had shown, especially in contrast to the Tories, that it had found the formula for peaceful and effective collectivist politics. The good cooperation during those first months seemed to confirm the party's faith in this goal.

The media were more sceptical. Columnists insisted that the social contract was a hoax which would do no more than buy a brief period of industrial peace.[15] They pointed out that the Government was delivering its part of the bargain first and that the unions therefore could renege on their responsibilities without fear of losing their gains.

The Government's record of accomplishment was indeed impressive during the first few months.

A. It ended restraints on collective bargaining, which included abolishing Stage II and the Pay Board, both the objects of special union criticism.

B. It continued a strengthened system of price controls including, as the TUC had demanded, controls on food and the payments of subsidies for food. Additionally, rents were frozen and new funds provided for expanding housing construction.

C. It increased pensions as agreed by the Liaison Committee.

D. It raised taxes for persons in the higher income brackets and closed loopholes for the wealthy.

E. It repealed the despised Industrial Relations Act and with it ended the infamous National Industrial Relations Court and the Commission on Industrial Relations.

F. It created the independent Arbitration and Conciliation Service as suggested by the Liaison Committee.

James Callaghan, then Foreign Secretary and one of the senior Labour leaders with the closest ties to the union movement, addressed the TUC Congress that September (1975) in triumph, but seeking payment for the party's IOU.[16] He reminded the delegates in rainy Brighton that they had reason to support the Labour Party again. Their help would be needed and expected in the coming election. Their help would also be needed and expected in delivering the wage restraint that the social contract had specified. In return, the Party promised to carry out the rest of the agreement in the next Parliament including the Employment Protection Act and legislation on industrial democracy. The basis had been laid, the Foreign Secretary told the delegates, for the social and economic reconstruction of our country.

Callaghan's speech also contained a warning that predicted the dominant economic theme in union–government relations for the following several years. The work of the Labour Government, he said, would be much more difficult because inflation was growing faster than at any time since the war. The fourfold oil price increases were having their impact. The brutal truth was that "people in many countries were now facing a temporary reduction in their standard of living".[17] While the problem of inflation was not new, the ferocity of this inflation would produce remedial policies which threatened to create very high unemployment. Callaghan warned: "I speak of nothing less than the prospect of a high level of unemployment, throughout the industrialized world, such as we have not seen since the 30s."[18]

Congress then delivered its nearly unanimous support for the social contract. The delegates voted not with Callaghan's chilling message in mind but because they were satisfied with the gains of Labour's first six months in office as well as the prospect of unrestrained collective bargaining in the coming year. Callaghan's warning was sobering but not more compelling at the time than the General Council's statement two months earlier encouraging unions to restrict wage demands to twelve-month intervals and to restrain the size of demands to ". . . compensation for the rise in the cost of living since the last settlement" or to the anticipated rise for the following year.[19] Within that caution, delegates found ample room for a return to free bargaining and certainly a pattern of wage negotiations which was far more agreeable than the statutory restraint of the Heath period. Few delegates suspected that within nine months "their" Government would rush to take drastic measures that would diminish their standards of living more than at any time since the depression forty years earlier.

Members of the General Council much better understood the importance of Callaghan's warning.[20] They had already wrestled with the conflicting pressures which on the one hand insisted that they take advantage of the new Government's hesitation to restrict collective bargaining, and on the other, insisted that they act "responsibly" to restrain wage claims.[21] Len Murray had frequently explained the danger that the oil crisis and gathering world recession posed to the British economy, especially in the midst of a domestic wage explosion. At the same time, though, union leaders

personally were very sympathetic to the shrill demands being made
by shop stewards that they move quickly to make up for the
distortions in wage differentials as well as the relative slippage of
wage purchasing power which Heath's restraint had produced.

The debate over these issues continued during the fall of 1974 and
into the spring of 1975. The union movement delivered its support
for Labour in the successful election of October 1974 which
returned the government with a small majority. But once Wilson
was reconfirmed in office, the policy debate heated up considerably.

Both wings of the Labour movement proceeded cautiously. They
were in complete agreement that whatever the intensity of crisis,
they would do everything to work out policy agreements that
avoided conflict between them. This meant that the Labour
Government watched in near silence during the last months of 1974
and into early 1975 as the size of wage settlements grew like Topsy.[22]
The miners settled for about 30 per cent and so too did the power
workers and railwaymen, but the Government soothingly commented each time that the agreements were within the social
contract. By the end of May 1975 average earnings stood nearly 29
per cent higher than they had been a year earlier.[23]

For its part, the TUC General Council suffered from con-
tradictary tensions. There was nervous discussion about the wage
explosion and its implications and yet even the most moderate
leaders pressed for increases that met the new "norms". Dramatic
crisis seemed imminent throughout these months as union leaders
could no longer refute the evidence that wage-push was contributing to roaring price inflation. Yet, as individual union leaders,
members of the General Council could find no other way to protect
their interests. Each in turn and especially those in the public sector
took up 30 per cent wage increases as their own bargaining goal.
Union leaders also felt compelled to act from their expectation that
the 1975 pay round would be the last under free bargaining for some
time to come. They viewed their efforts to "get as much as possible"
not simply as greedy expedience but as hedging against prospective
hard times.[24]

The General Council continued to muddle through in this
atmosphere during the early months of 1975.[25] Len Murray issued
statements at the end of nearly every General Council and
Economic Committee meeting bravely applauding the social
contract in much the same synthetic terms as the Government used
in accepting each ever-larger wage agreement.[26] But the strain

increasingly showed through. Murray's statements constantly reminded unions about the TUC's voluntary restraint policy. The General Secretary also took each opportunity to remind the Government that the TUC took a special interest in maintaining employment levels and preventing the erosion of living standards. But by the late spring even the TUC could not ignore the obvious problem.

The figures on unemployment and inflation in March and then especially in April were decisive. Unemployment jumped by more than 100,000 to nearly 900,000 in April, which compared very badly with the low of just over 500,000 during the previous June and 600,000 at the time of the last Congress.[27] Figures for price inflation were just as bad. The rate of annual increase in March, taking the three previous months as the basis, was 27.7 per cent, and in April it was 33 per cent.[28]

The general alarm throughout the country was compelling. Prices were rising at a rate which caused highly visible changes weekly. The rise in unemployment extended beyond very young school-leavers and older workers. Discontent poured into the TUC and the seriousness of the economic situation provided a sense of urgency not seen at Congress House since the fuel shortage of 1947.[29]

POWER MOVES TO THE POLITICAL SIDE: A RETURN TO INCOME POLICY

Jack Jones was the key TUC figure in prodding the General Council to take the initiative. Jones and Michael Foot, the Employment Secretary, were on very close terms from the beginning of the Labour Government.[30] They worked together closely on the social contract and continued to serve as the key access persons for each side in monitoring the arrangement, especially between meetings of the Liaison Committee. It was therefore quite natural that their conversations provided the major point of dialogue between the unions and government about the growing economic problems during early 1975. Other TUC leaders certainly played significant roles in this dialogue, as did James Callaghan. However, Michael Foot more than any other Minister worked regularly with trade unionists and his long identity with union interests endowed him with a special legitimacy for TUC leaders.[31]

Jones learned most about the growing crisis and worry in the Cabinet during those early months of 1975. Foot feared progressively higher wage settlements. Jones in return cautioned against Government measures which would pose a deflationary threat to union interests. Both men communicated regularly back to their colleagues.

In April 1975 it was Jones who took the first steps in trying to convince the General Council to act pre-emptively. Len Murray very much agreed with his approach. The danger that the social contract might disintegrate and ultimately threaten the incumbency of this Labour Government were serious matters which the union movement could not afford to risk.

Jones was thoroughly proud of the social contract. He believed that it not only provided tangible gains for union interests but also built renewed support for the political alliance which looked so tattered in 1969.[32] Moreover, there was significant hope for the future. The Labour Government was committed now to carry on with the task of building the sort of egalitarian and just society which Jones enthusiastically supported. His optimism contrasted sharply with his cynical expectations about a future Tory Government. The bitterness of 1974 still hung heavily over that relationship and Jones believed that matters would get still worse under a government headed by Margaret Thatcher, who seemed to be committed to avoid even the slightest influential consultations with the union movement.

At bottom, though, Jones pointed to the self-interest of trade unionists in stemming price inflation. The figures were now quite shocking and it was apparent to him, as well as to others on the General Council, that hyperinflation carried ugly consequences that could not be tolerated. However much leverage some unions might swing in the bargaining process, they could not keep up with prices that rose weekly. And for weaker unions, which included sections of his own Transport Union, hyperinflation would be a disaster. It was clear by April that wage rises were slipping rapidly behind the pace of price rises, with every indication that this gap would grow in the months ahead.

Jones produced a plan for wage restraint with these fears clearly in mind. He proposed that the General Council agree that the size of pay increases be limited to £6 per week, with no increase for those making over £7000 per year – if the unions, employers and the Government could work out a "suitable" arrangement for price control.[33] This plan would operate on a completely voluntary basis under a commitment by the Government to avoid statutory action or sanctions of any kind. Jones also insisted that the Government make an additional commitment to resume reflationary economic policies and the extension of social programmes at the first feasible moment. He assumed, moreover, that the Government would not take advantage of this period of restraint in order to impose the sort of large-scale deflationary programmes which Labour and Conservative Governments had imposed in the past.

Ministers were generally delighted and relieved by the Jones plan.[34] They had worried about the need for wage restraint for some time but had found no way to overcome their political inhibition against pressing the TUC. Their best chance for subtle influence throughout was the Jones–Foot dialogue and it worked much better than anyone had dared to hope.

The General Council was more divided over the plan. Moderates and right-wing members clearly believed that Jones had produced a sensible approach. They agreed that the time had arrived for a union initiative that would head off a breakdown in the social contract or possible Government policies which might cut living standards or increase unemployment.[35] They believed that union interests would be much better served if the TUC administered the bitter medicine itself than if the Government tried to impose it. The crisis was another testing time; the TUC should act immediately to maximize its leverage rather than vainly fight against reality which would ultimately require unpleasant remedial policies anyway.

Militant elements on the Council argued in reply against any policy which gave away the right to free bargaining. They complained that once again a Labour Government was unfairly asking the union partners to bear the costs of the nation's problems.[36] Not only did they believe it wholly unjust to blame price inflation on wage inflation, but they believed that the burden for remedial measures should fall far more heavily on the well-off. This argument was familiar, but it still carried much weight because restraint during the Heath period worked against the standard of living as prices kept rising despite wage restraint. And now, with price inflation moving up toward 30 per cent, it seemed especially important for unions to protect their members through a free collective bargaining process.

The argument was finally settled in June in favour of TUC action. The situation became so critical that few on the Council continued to believe that the Government would hesitate to act for very much longer. The Council finally agreed therefore on six general points about the direction that the social contract should take during the following year. At its June meeting, the General Council agreed that:[37]

1. A price target should be set and achieved by the middle of 1976;
2. "A figure for pay, related to the achievement of this [price] target in the form of a flat money increase, [should be] universally applied";[38]
3. There should be limits on very high incomes;
4. There should be radical action to limit price increases, involving application of the Price Code, subsidies and action at High Street level;
5. There should be a major reduction in 1976 in unemployment levels;
6. There should be continuation of the social contract as the basis for unity between the union movement and the Labour Government.

The General Council left the final terms of the agreement open to subsequent negotiations with the CBI and the Government. However, events moved more rapidly than the talks. On 30 June a 1.3 per cent fall in the value of the pound precipitated a sharp crisis. By the next afternoon, Dennis Healey told the House of Commons that the TUC and CBI needed urgently to reach agreement to reduce inflation.[39] He said that the government would work towards a 10 per cent inflation rate initially and to single figures by the end of 1976. He further suggested that the increase in wages and salaries during the next round be limited to 10 per cent, as should dividends. Finally, he suggested that "there should be cash limits for wage bills in the public sector and action through the Price Code in the private sector".[40]

The Chancellor went out of his way that afternoon to praise the recent TUC decision to support limits on wages and prices. He said that he much preferred to continue following this voluntary approach although the Government would need to legislate if there was no substantial agreement. Such legislation would not apply to employees this time but rather to employers, who would be prohibited from making agreements which exceeded the 10 per cent limit.

Working under the pressure of the Chancellor's warning that he would act, the TUC and CBI met with Government Ministers for the next week and a half. The Government held the real advantage that both the union and employer representatives were fully convinced that the crisis was every bit as serious as the Chancellor had portrayed.[41] On 9 July the TUC published its formal views in a pamphlet *The Development of the Social Contract*.[42] Two days later, the Government published the White Paper, *The Attack on Inflation*, which presented the official policy to meet the crisis, incorporating the TUC's suggestions as well as the fruits of the "tripartite" talks which had just concluded.[43]

The White Paper is an especially interesting document when viewed as an indication of the changing relationship between the TUC and the Labour Government at that time. No government statement before had so explicitly claimed the TUC's influence. In every section the Government acknowledged either that it had taken the TUC's views into account or that it had directly adopted its proposals. The £6 pay limit, for example, was taken over by the Government directly and the relevant passage on pay from the TUC's own published proposals was attached as an annex to the White Paper.[44] In addition, the Government adopted a whole series of buffering measures that met the TUC demand that the Government soften the harshest impact that the recession would have on the living standards of working people. Food subsidies were continued and raised and rent increases held to the level of general price inflation. As for unemployment, the Government promised to introduce a temporary employment subsidy to help compensate employers for maintaining employees who would have otherwise been laid off.

These measures in sum represented a considerable acknowledgement of the continuing power of the union movement, and the perceptions of Ministers that they needed TUC cooperation in order to make incomes policy work. But there could be no mistaking the significance of the policy that the White Paper announced. The Labour Government had broken through the taboo against incomes policy which stood as a cornerstone of union–Labour relations ever since the defeat of *In Place of Strife*. The growing fears at Congress House about the economy withered TUC resistance. Events sapped union strength and the Government took the advantage, however much its buffering measures "sweetened" the bitter medicine.

The TUC Congress in September 1975 was the last hurdle in ratifying the policy. Congress was supportive, though with some misgivings.[45] The level of disagreement closely approximated the 19–13 vote by which the General Council in early July approved its own proposals which became central to the White Paper.[46] But the arguments against the policy were weak when compared to the stridently anti-incomes policy debates at Congress during the late sixties. Hugh Scanlon's engineers remained intransigent though the other large TUC unions unanimously supported the General Council–Government position.

Leverage thus passed to the political side of the Labour movement as the £6 pay policy began its year-long run. From the time of that summer's TUC Congress nearly every member of the General Council became convinced that Britain's economic situation was so dangerous that there was no alternative but to support the Government's economic policies. They demanded some mutuality of cooperation which the Government delivered in the form of additional palliative selective measures, but in the main they acted timidly out of pure fear.

The situation was broadly similar to 1947 when the Labour Government won the only other example of effective union cooperation for wage restraint. A sudden fuel crisis finally convinced a reluctant General Council to acquiesce in the Attlee Government's pleadings for restraint. That Government too had earned a considerable amount of union goodwill by fulfilling its promises to introduce a thorough programme of economic and social reforms. But fear was at the root of cooperation then as in 1975. It was a fear that Labour's failure would open the door for a new Conservative Government and with it a return to deprivation. The fuel crisis in 1947 was a compelling stimulant for cooperation because it caused three million workers to lose their jobs within a very few days. The spectre of renewed depression produced fear enough at that time to convince the General Council to agree to a wage freeze which held firmly for nearly 18 months.

Len Murray argued in much the same terms at the 1975 Congress in urging that the General Council's recommendations on the £6 pay policy be accepted. Murray told the delegates that the General Council had no choice. Britain, he said, faced three crises:

There is the world recession. There is the crisis of domestic

inflation, which is very high even by international standards. And
there is the crisis of industrial obsolescence, which is the most
deep-seated crisis of all. . . . Our dilemma is that we have to
tackle these three problems simultaneously. The stark reality is
that some people, for a time, are going to have some reduction in
their living standards. I do not want to burke that issue.[47]

The fact is, he went on, "in recent months increases in incomes have
been the primary cause of rising prices. Whatever else needs to be
done . . . we cannot deny that some action is needed on the pay
front."[48] He told the delegates that he had been long nurtured on
the argument that the best way to protect employment was to pump
purchasing power into the economy. "And a very good line of
argument it is – when the circumstances are appropriate. But what
would be the purpose now of pushing up incomes? . . . You know
what the consequences of that would be. It would only push prices
up faster."[49]

The trade union movement had no recourse now, he continued,
but to put its faith in the Government. The unions need to accept
pay restraint and trust this Government, which had already
delivered so much, to take the lead in accomplishing what trade
unionists most wanted: to protect employment, to foster a return to
growth and rises in the standard of living. For the year ahead, the
goals would be to halt and then reduce the level of price inflation,
and to halt and then reduce the level of unemployment. Murray
urged the delegates to that Congress to accept pay restraint as a
straightforward trade-off. And in the interim while unemployment
remained high and prices high, the TUC would also press the
Government to provide selective measures which would at least
buffer working people somewhat, especially young people, from the
worst of the recession.

COOPERATION FROM WEAKNESS

The TUC thought it had agreed to a palatable arrangement and for
about a year its judgement looked sound. Events, however, overtook
this equilibrium and worked decidedly to the union movement's
disadvantage. The economic situation deteriorated in a succession
of crises which prompted the Government to tighten its deflationary
policies. The bite of recession was harder than Healey had first

predicted but the TUC could find no alternative to its fidelity to the initial agreement and faith in the Labour Government.

The first year proceeded very much as originally agreed, with little hint of the trouble to come. The Economic Committee consulted regularly with the Chancellor to monitor the conduct of the agreement. The TUC retained throughout this period the most intimate access to Government departments and Ministers on a daily basis. Quite early in the year a pattern of trade-offs developed between both sides. The TUC studiously kept its bargain on wage restraint while the Chancellor responded favourably to a succession of TUC demands for remedial policies designed to save as many jobs as possible and otherwise soften the effects of the decline in the standard of living.[50] The arrangement worked so well that the agreement held firm even in the face of seriously worsening unemployment during the winter and spring of 1976.[51]

One typical example of the trade-off pattern which was repeated a number of times during the year occurred a few weeks after Congress in late September and October, 1975.[52] The Chancellor responded to favourable support at Congress by announcing a package of measures. He provided £75 million more for training and boosted public spending on construction by £30 million in addition to providing other aid to industry totalling £80 million.

The General Council in turn applauded the Chancellor's moves, congratulating itself for the Government's acceptance of its advice. Two months later, in December, the Council offered the Government another batch of recommendations including suggestions that the Government adopt import controls; spend more on public housing including repairs and maintenance; build up stocks of steel; extend the time coverage for the Temporary Employment Subsidy; and pay a £10 bonus to pensioners.[53] Chancellor Healey again took up most of these suggestions in a second announcement.

This pattern worked so well that there was little doubt at the beginning of 1976 that the TUC would agree to a second year of restraint in some form. The very moderate and cooperative tone of the *Economic Review*, published in February, confirmed the continued rapport.[54] The TUC explicitly recognized that the economic situation was still worsening and that the steady fall in the value of the pound made "son of £6 limit" inevitable. This understanding attitude continued even after the Chancellor turned down the TUC's request for a very modest reflation in his budget. Instead, the TUC quietly accepted yet another package of selective measures.

There is no better example of this close working arrangement than the smooth way in which talks proceeded during the spring of 1976 toward a second formal agreement for voluntary restraint. Len Murray participated in an almost continuous dialogue with the Chancellor and Michael Foot during these weeks. The Chancellor in his budget, moreover, helped to play a very carefully orchestrated scenario which was designed to bolster the TUC's image as responsible protector of union interests even while it agreed to a second year of restraint.[55]

In this scenario the Chancellor offered a package of conditional tax relief. He promised to increase personal allowances by £60 for single persons, by £130 for married persons and increase the rate of tax thresholds by £500 – if the TUC would agree to a pay guideline that did not exceed 3 per cent for the coming year. The General Council caustically denounced this percentage as ridiculous but then entered into negotiations from which it emerged "triumphantly" with a figure of 5 per cent, including an extension of the 12-month rule for increases.[56]

The General Council subsequently held a Special Congress on 16 June to ratify this agreement. The delegates were unusually docile. Even Hugh Scanlon dropped his opposition, openly admitting and urging the delegates to accept that the TUC could do no better in this period when living standards were likely to fall even more. Scanlon told the Congress in a revealing passage:

> Why do most people now come to a conclusion that we have to support the General Council? I say first and foremost because we believe the general strategy of the Government is correct, with its emphasis that if Britain is to get out of the undoubted economic difficulties, she can only do it on the basis of a viable, efficient manufacturing industry with emphasis on those who make and sell and, if necessary, somewhat less emphasis on those who serve. That is point one of the strategy.
>
> The second point is to work in cooperation and not in confrontation with the trade union Movement, and to try and work out plans and strategies in the industrial, political and legislative fields. I say without fear of contradiction not that it has achieved all that we wanted it to do – and I will make some remarks in that regard in respect of our own negotiations – but that it has striven manfully to try and achieve it against a House of Commons which seems determined either to destroy itself or

perhaps in the process hold up the whole of the strategy not only to ridicule but to try and make it impossible to achieve. That is why at this moment in time it is necessary for this trade union Movement to speak and, I would hope, to speak with one voice in order to try and get such a strategy fulfilled.[57]

PAIN AND MORE PAIN

Within a month Scanlon and others began to rue their soothing words about the benevolent direction of Government policy. On 14 July the new Prime Minister, James Callaghan, along with his Chancellor, Dennis Healey, told dismayed members of the Economic Committee that the Government had decided to make significantly larger cuts in public expenditure than they had first announced in February.[58] Their purpose was to head off another run on the pound which they believed would otherwise begin very shortly.

These measures took the Committee by surprise, and most unpleasantly so. As events were to show, the 14 July meeting proved to be the beginning of a series of sudden Government moves which undercut the terms of its relationship with the TUC and undercut union power as well. The Committee objected to the proposed action because public expenditure levels strongly affected their member's economic prospects as well as because the Government had failed to consult it before taking this decision.

Public expenditure was an especially sensitive issue since the TUC and the Government had argued during the previous winter over the terms of a White Paper published in February.[59] That Paper had announced that expenditures would remain at current levels until 1980, allowing only for increases due to inflation. The TUC vocally worried at the time that such restraints would doom all possibility that unemployment could be reduced significantly as the Government had earlier promised. The July cuts therefore meant in the TUC's view that unemployment would necessarily remain at present low levels, with no hope of any reduction. Such a change obviously struck at the main underpinnings of the social contract.[60]

The hard words that were exchanged that afternoon were therefore inevitable. The Chancellor tried without much success to convince the Committee that the Government had no alternative in the face of a likely new run on the pound.[61] He said that public sector deficits simply could not continue at the present levels because such spending would ultimately destroy the Government's investment and inflation policies by driving up interest rates and increasing the money supply. In that event, he warned, the Government would be forced to borrow abroad or from the International Monetary Fund under terms which would be most unpleasant.

The Committee wasn't impressed with this argument. It asked for a few days time to develop a formal substantive reply to the Chancellor, but in the meantime several members indicated that they were very sceptical. Moreover, they were extremely unhappy about the way that the Government "sprung" this latest crisis on them. Several Committee members wondered out loud what all the hurry was about. After all, when the TUC objected to the earlier White Paper on public expenditures during the winter the Chancellor promised that he would allow more time for consultations on the subject in the future.

The Committee met with the Chancellor again two days later on 16 July.[62] By then its members were ready with a strong case against the Government's position. They insisted that industry would indeed have adequate financing to sustain an economic recovery. The new round of cuts therefore would only produce more unemployment without doing any good. Worse, though, the Committee argued that there could be no assurance that foreign speculators would be impressed with these measures.

The argument went unresolved that day. Three days later, on 19 July, the Economic Committee sent a formal written statement to the Chancellor re-emphasizing the points it had made in the two sessions.[63] Included in the statement was the caution that the Government should not overlook union views: "It should not need emphasis that the confidence of the trade union Movement in the course of economic policy is of equal weight to the need for confidence on the part of the financial community at home and abroad."[64]

The TUC's arguments and warning had little effect on the Chancellor's policy, which he announced three days later on 22 July. [65] The cuts in public expenditures amounted to £1 billion and the employer's national insurance contribution was raised by 2 per cent, which had the total effect of reducing the public sector borrowing requirement by about £1.5 billion to £9 billion. In addition, Healey announced other measures which struck directly at union interests: the further relaxation of the price code; increased charges on school meals and various health services; more rapid phasing out of food subsidies; cuts in road construction and improvements; and even reductions in funding for educational programmes. The direct effect on employment was to be the loss of 60,000 jobs.

The General Council was obviously very unhappy about the cuts as well as its own inability to deter the Chancellor. Some members charged that they had been deceived into agreeing to a second year of restraint. But after considerable argument among themselves, the Council decided to do no more than publish their 19 July letter to the Chancellor.

Gloom laced with resignation dominated the speeches given by General Council members at Congress a little more than a month later in September 1976.[66] Public-sector unions most vocally objected that the Government was reneging on its part of the Social Contract.[67] Len Murray in reply argued, as he had in June, that the union movement needed to understand that the Government and the country were in a difficult situation: "The fact is that we can only afford a decent level of public spending if we achieve a healthy, growing economy based ultimately on improving our manufacturing investment."[68] Hugh Scanlon followed the same approach, demonstrating that he was sticking with the Government.[69] David Basnett spoke in much the same terms.[70] All agreed that the Government could still count on union cooperation. They could see no alternative at the moment. The Government should be careful not to take them for granted but otherwise they promised that they would soldier on.

The TUC had the bitter satisfaction in the months ahead of watching its worst fears come true. Sterling plummeted during the fall of 1976 despite the Government's cuts in public expenditure. By October the pound was at an all-time low of $1.55 and the devaluation against all other major currencies was 48 per cent.

Once again the Chancellor produced a batch of deflationary measures designed to stem the outflow of reserves. He also announced that the Government would immediately seek a large loan from the International Monetary Fund while it simultaneously acted against the growth in the money supply with the intention of driving the current 20 per cent growth rate down to no more than 12 per cent.[71] Peter Jay, in commenting on this action, put the

Chancellor's moves into a perspective which the trade union leadership was bound to dislike: "The fact remains that the consequences of yesterday's decisions are likely to be extremely severe. Monetary restraint is not a soft way of achieving the disinflationary effects of fiscal restraints without the disagreeable disinflationary impact on the real economy . . . There must therefore be a question whether even this form of counter-inflationary policy can withstand the political pressures which resentment against high unemployment and disappointing living standards naturally causes."[72]

Three days after his announcement, Healey met with the TUC's top team, the six members of the National Economic Development Council.[73] The meeting was part of a regular schedule of discussions between the unions and Government, but this meeting took on special importance in view of the government's measures. The TUC side included Len Murray, Jack Jones, Hugh Scanlon, Daniel McGarvey, David Basnett, and Lord Allen. The Government side included Healey, Roy Hattersley, Secretary of State for Prices and Consumer Protection, and Albert Booth, the Employment Secretary. Once again, as in July, the TUC complained that it had not been adequately consulted about a policy initiative which it strongly opposed. Inter-staff contact did provide advance information but the Chancellor did not provide enough time for what the TUC described as influential consultations. The TUC angrily criticized the Chancellor's moves, insisting that he had introduced new tension into the social contract relationship. Unionists were being asked once again to continue their wage restraint while prices grew rapidly without chance of significant control and without much hope that improvement of the economy in the following months would forestall another lurch downward in the standard of living. The TUC added that it was particularly concerned that the impending negotiations with the IMF would produce terms which made the outlook even more bleak. They complained that in fact the most worrying element of the present announcement was that it appeared that the Government had already been won over to the monetarist argument.

TUC representatives repeated these same points two weeks later when they met with the Prime Minister.[74] Len Murray repeated them for a third time with considerable bitterness when he met with IMF officials to discuss Britain's loan application.[75] All had little effect even though the Cabinet approved the loan terms only after serious argument. There was enormous frustration at Congress House at the TUC's lack of influence. The Government seemed very distracted by the demands being made abroad by the IMF, and by the United States as well as the EEC. The final IMF loan terms seemed to confirm another year of recession: Britain would receive a £2.3 billion loan but in return for public expenditure cuts totalling £1 billion in 1977 and a further £1.5 billion in 1978–79.[76]

Just after the Chancellor announced his "IMF mini-budget" and just before Christmas of 1976 senior TUC leaders went to Downing Street to review the economic situation.[77] It was a sad and frustrating occasion for both sides. There was no negotiation, just discussion and contemplation about the year just ending and the prospects for 1977. There were no recriminations about what had happened. But everyone recognized that there had been little progress in spite of enormous sacrifices. The fall in sterling during the spring and then precipitously during the fall ensured that the sacrifice of wage restraints so well kept by the unions would little reduce inflation. Inflation was still running at more than 15 per cent though the Chancellor had promised that it would by then be down to under 10 per cent.[78] Unemployment, which had quickly surged to 1.5 million, still hovered at that figure, with signs of worsening again in the new year.[79] Finally, the balance of payments, which Healey had expected to improve markedly by then, was instead in greater deficit because the falling price of sterling made British imports so much more expensive.

The stark facts in sum were that the trade-offs built into the social contracts had yielded nothing better than a poor holding action. High prices, high unemployment, a poor balance of payments, a falling standard of living was the spectacle, only relieved by some evidence that the situation would have been considerably worse had it not been for the success of wage restraint. And the prospect from that Christmas meeting for the following year was only for more sacrifice.

ACQUIESCENCE: 1977–78

This soul-searching at Number 10 was eye-opening for members of the General Council. Review of the frustrations and failures of 1976 crystallized their growing concern that the social contract was working very strongly against them.[80] Their dilemma remained

unchanged after another year of sacrifice: recession was obviously
sapping the power of trade unionism but recovery, which would be
likely to bring renewed influence was still elusively beyond the
horizon. In the meantime their best hope for positive change
remained in cooperating with this Labour Government, whose
policies were much less kindly to union interests than the General
Council certainly would have liked.[81]

But what to do? The best the General Council could hope for in
this gloomy situation was to improve the terms of the relationship,
but it needed to do so with real care that conflict between the TUC
and the Government should not go so far as to endanger the
incumbency of Callaghan's minority administration. The Tories
remained menacingly ahead in the polls and seemed only too
eager to return to office carrying their less benevolent attitude
toward the unions. Memories of 1974 still burned deep at the TUC.

The approach that the General Council developed from this view
and early in 1977 can best be described as "acquiescence". The
general framework of cooperation with the Government remained
firmly intact, but the TUC took a much less agreeable posture
toward government policy in specific terms.[82] Very early in the
year, for example, Len Murray told the Prime Minister that the
TUC would not agree to a third year of *formal* restraint unless the
Government delivered considerably more beneficial incentives.

The *Economic Review* in February added to this approach by
heavily criticizing the Government's failure to do more to protect
living standards and diminish unemployment.[83] Abandoning the
timidity of the 1976 Report, the *Review* demanded a large economic
reflation. The TUC insisted that the Government pump £2.4
billion into the economy in this effort. A few weeks later the
Economic Committee protested again when the Chancellor suggested that he would guarantee only £500 million in reflation but
add another £1 million if the TUC would accept a third round of
wage restraint. Lord Allen and his colleagues told the Chancellor
that they weren't about to do a deal for so little in return.[84] There
would be no agreement beyond the simple extension of the 12-
month gap between wage settlements unless the Government
sweetened its offer considerably.

Talks throughout the balance of the spring in fact did not
produce any agreement. Lord Allen and Len Murray privately
reassured the Prime Minister and his Chancellor that the TUC
understood the importance of their policies but that there was no

way they could lead their men into another year of restraint.[85] The TUC, in sum, could acquiesce to a great extent in the Government's policies but it could no longer formally cooperate without substantial return.

By July the Government recognized and acquiesced in the trade union position, not wanting itself to precipitate a damaging conflict. The White Paper accordingly announced, even hailed, a return to free bargaining while laying down the Government's own view that earnings should be held to no more than 10 per cent for the coming year, though without the formal arrangement that had operated during the previous two years.[86]

The TUC Congress in September confirmed this arrangement and the "marriage" between the two sides of the labour movement proceeded intact but on a new basis. The Government, for its part, liked to refer to the period after 1 August, as Stage Three. The TUC insisted that the White Paper had best described the year as a time for the orderly return to free collective bargaining. Either way, acquiescence worked well throughout the balance of 1977 and into 1978, as the economy showed signs of real financial recovery and a declining rate of inflation, even though output remained stagnant.[87]

Acquiescence – on both sides – continued to describe best the relationship in 1978. The TUC made it clear even earlier and more forcefully that it would not agree to a formal Stage Four restraint. The Government only briefly tried to win more formal cooperation. By the early spring the Callaghan Cabinet became resigned to another year of informal restraint coupled with the TUC's general promise of goodwill in the effort to press for economic recovery.[88] In July, the Government again announced an informal guideline or norm for earnings increases in the year from 1 August. This time the figure was lowered 10 per cent to 5 per cent. But the signals from the rank and file were clear: they would rebel against further severe restraint. Two years of discipline threatened to break down into renewed wage conflict during the next pay round in early 1979.

CONCLUSION

The most salient assessment about the relationship between the unions and the Labour Government beginning in 1974 was that it was cooperative to a remarkable degree. It was cooperative primarily to the union's advantage between February 1974 and

June 1975. After that through the middle of 1978, the time of this writing, it was cooperative primarily to the advantage of the political side of the Labour movement in Government. Once again, the special familial ties between the union movement and the Labour Party impinged very strongly.

These examples at first glance would seem to confirm at least in a modified way Harold Wilson's famous boast during the 1964 election that only the Labour Party can command the cooperation of the union movement by its special relationship. But Wilson at that time was boasting that a Labour Government could command such loyalty in any circumstance and particularly for a cooperative, positive effort to develop economic prosperity. The experiences of the last four years, however, still leave Wilson's confidence unproved. The cooperation between unions and Government from 1974 was rooted once again in mutual fear and defensiveness, just as in 1947.

This assessment is both optimistic as well as worrying. There has been cooperation – and that development deserves an optimistic review. By 1974, when Labour returned to office in the midst of the miners' strike, there was no shortage of political and media comment that the experience of first the Wilson and then the Heath Government demonstrated that cooperation between the unions and government in the management of the economy was impossible. This pessimism proved untrue. The Wilson Government skilfully rekindled the union stake in the labour alliance by loyally implementing the policies worked out by the Liaison Committe beginning in 1970. After 1975, with Britain in full-blown recession, the Government again skilfully drew on its earned credibility with the unions, themselves gripped with fear, to develop a remarkably successful wage restraint policy which many analysts in July 1975 had prematurely written off as a pipe-dream.

The worrying element, demonstrated again by industrial conflict in early 1979, is that union–Labour Party cooperation is still an unproven possibility in less than crisis conditions. The same basic dilemma which intruded to destroy collectivist relationships during the sixties remains a serious potential in more "normal" economic conditions. Trade unions are still basically committed to getting more and better terms of employment for their members. We have, as yet, no solid evidence that they would be willing to sacrifice this purpose while accepting a Government-defined sense of "responsibility" to the national interest, which usually means an incomes policy. It thus remains a crucial problem for the Labour Party, and no less for the Conservatives, who have never achieved cooperation with the unions in any period, to find some means of reproducing the sort of cooperation which Labour enjoyed during two periods under nearly siege conditions.

5 Beyond Paralysis: British Trade Unionism in the European Communities

The British polity at the end of the seventies still confronts the problem of integrating the new and powerful functional representatives into the existing political system. The specific argument between the trade union movement and governments of both parties about what role and influence this largest functional entity shall play in the management of the economy remains unsolved. Except for periods of extreme crisis with Labour in power, as since 1974, the outcome of union–government conflicts has nearly always been the paralysis of economic policy. Unions have repeatedly vetoed policies to which they objected, thus leaving government to develop ineffective alternatives which have tended to recycle the basic problems which government has tried to solve.

This still-unresolved dilemma has aroused considerable frustration as well as a search for a "way out", for some formula that can break the pattern of collectivist paralysis.[1] One tantalizing possibility is that British membership in the European Communities may transfer significant economic decision-making to Brussels where there may develop a more productive and cooperative relationship. Short of the wholesale transfer of significant power, however, there is also the possibility that a new combination of interaction may operate to break the internal British impasse. For example, EEC economic issues might identify coinciding national interests, encouraging a greater dimension of cooperation between British unions and British government. There is also a contrasting possibility that British membership may give British government new leverage against the unions. In this kind of scenario the British government would be able to dangle its support as a spokesman for British interests in the Council of Ministers and in other EEC institutions as the price for union cooperation at home.

Until recently these possibilities or some variant on them seemed fanciful. The future of British membership in the EEC was uncertain before the referendum in 1975. For its part, the TUC simply ignored the EEC, even refusing after accession in 1973 to fill the seats on various Community bodies to which it was entitled. The TUC in these years exercised so much power at home in Britain that it could find little to gain from participating in Europe.

The bite of severe economic crisis, with the fall in the standard of living and especially the rise of unemployment, dramatically altered the picture. The strains of economic recession began in 1975 to weaken seriously the props of union strength which had endured over the last three decades. Much as full employment conferred power and gave the unions a stake in the *status quo*, unemployment has sapped that power and encouraged unions to support change – at least change that enhances their interests. Thus, unemployment has produced strong demands from constituent unions for powerful TUC leadership in winning remedial government policies, just as the TUC in better times was expected to win government acquiescence in union efforts to use the full measure of free collective bargaining in order to secure higher and higher wages.

In the past, the TUC responded to cyclical recessions by forcefully reminding government that it had an obligation to carry out the 1944 all-party commitment to preserve full employment as a first economic priority. The TUC's long-held attitude was that government reflation of the economy was a matter of choice. Accordingly, Tory governments that hesitated to reflate were accused of acting out their class biases while Labour governments were accused of infidelity and thought to have been seduced by Treasury mandarins and international bankers.

The hardest lesson for union leaders and especially for TUC economists in recent years has therefore been the link between inflation and unemployment. They have come to accept in searching for new strategies that reflation is no longer the simple solution to Britain's problems.[2]

In sum, the General Council of the TUC for several years now has been facing a pessimistic situation. Domestic political and economic options are limited, while the intrusion of external economic imperatives and the force of economic interdependence during the recession have become more and more obvious. It is hardly surprising then that beginning during the last half of 1975 the General Council started to explore the European possibilities.

I THE MOVE INTO EUROPE

The TUC's interest in Europe is defensive. It has sought from the beginning both to protect the standard of living of its membership as well as its role as a powerful force in economic decision-making. Its long battle against the EEC in Britain was undertaken largely because the TUC worried that British membership would undermine its own influence.[3] The irony in 1975 was that these fears were becoming reality. The TUC's move into Europe beginning in that year therefore indicated that from the TUC's perspective the British domestic economic and political situation had so eroded as to compel it to take this initiative despite the well-considered risks that European unity might hold for the future.

The General Council also recognized that its move into Europe at that time was directed primarily at influencing the policies of other European national governments far more than the Community itself.[4] TUC leaders did not believe for a moment that the EEC yet had very great impact by its own policies. Rather, they were impressed with the force of economic interdependence and especially the effect of European economic conduct on the British economy.

The TUC carried many policy goals into Europe. The central focus has been unemployment. Some policies, especially the selective or micro-economic policies, were already agreed with the British government in the Social Contract and the TUC is hoping to internationalize them. Others, and the most important to the TUC, are macro-economic, including policies which the TUC cannot win at home, or otherwise reflect its awareness that changes in macro-economic policies abroad can be helpful to the British domestic economy. Most of the macro-economic policy goals are national rather than Community. The most important of both include:[5]

1. Community targets for re-establishing full employment, reducing inflation, and promoting economic growth. These targets should then be used by national governments, based on their own economic strengths, to adopt specific policies. One major TUC aim is to convince the German government to lead the general recovery and reflation because it, more than any other country, is healthy enough and large enough to encourage by its spending the return of solid demand in Britain.

2. Specific programmes to protect existing jobs and create new ones. The TUC is anxious to have other countries adopt the British form of temporary employment subsidies, regional employment subsidies, expansion of the construction industry, longer vacations, shorter hours, and earlier retirement for workers along with programmes of public works projects.

3. Community use of the social and regional funds and the European Investment Bank in ways that will be more helpful in relieving unemployment.

4. Community harmonization upward of unemployment compensation programmes.

5. Community coordination of national policies that maximize employment.

6. Community leadership in pressing a dynamic trade programme, with special leadership in working out long-term natural resource agreements with developing countries.

7. Community leadership in creating more stable currency patterns.

II THE PROBLEM OF ACCESS IN EUROPE

The TUC's major challenge in Europe has not been in deciding what its policy goals are, but in learning how it can achieve them. This problem is especially frustrating for so powerful a functional group experienced in direct contact with the British government on a daily basis. The TUC in Europe, by contrast, usually finds itself communicating through less sympathetic third parties or through cumbersome bureaucratic machinery. The major channels of access are:

1. Through institutions in which the TUC participates directly as a national representative, such as the Economic and Social Committee;

2. Through institutions, such as the specialized committees and conferences, in which the TUC is represented indirectly by the European Trades Union Confederation (ETUC);

3. Through institutions in which the British government must represent TUC interests, such as the Council.

A. THE EUROPEAN TRADES UNION CONFEDERATION (ETUC)

The ETUC is the TUC of Europe and as such offers the TUC its best access to European unions and their possible support on issues such as unemployment. The potential importance of this help could be very great if European unions vigorously pressed their own governments while acting together to stress European policies. The prospects suggested by historical experience, however, look less bright. Unions in European countries have individually been less influential than the TUC in Britain. Collective action has proved virtually impossible to organize and when achieved has made little impact. The value of the ETUC as an effective interest group is therefore questionable, though since the ETUC was founded only a few years ago and unemployment is its first vital issue it is too early to reach a clear assessment.

The TUC has been closely involved in the development of the ETUC from the start and was firmly committed to trying for more than five years to build a European union organization that could overcome the traditional obstacles to union collectivism: excessive nationalism and ideological incompatibility. The orginal incentive for the TUC in developing the ETUC was its interest in finding ways of dealing with multinational corporations. Very soon, however, the possibility that Britain would join the EEC made the effort even more important, although the TUC always insisted, and with success, that the ETUC include EFTA as well as EEC countries.

The problems of intergrating trade unionism on a European scale are much more difficult, it must be emphasized, than building a powerful national trade union organization. Differences of ex-perience, priorities, national environment, and organizational strengths are all complicating factors. For example, while all unions share a common commitment to full employment, their commit-ments may stand at different levels in the range of each national organization's priorities. The TUC exhibits the especially strong British fear of unemployment; the depression during the 1920s with its political consequences has had its effect. But the Germans are very much more fearful of inflation and in the category of special sensitivities the German unions' fear of inflation matches the British fear of unemployment. These different priorities inevitably produce differences in policy outlook.

Another example of complicating differences are the relative national strengths and organizational successes of each national trade union movement. The TUC is easily the largest and most powerful body among all the members of the ETUC. It is not surprising, therefore, that the TUC has also been the most vigorous and optimistic about developing a powerful ETUC. By comparison, French unions are less aggressive and more pessimistic, largely because their experience is filled with more disappointments. Historically, French unions have been weak, both because they are divided over ideology and because they have been able to organize only about half the proportion of working people that the TUC represents.

In spite of these problems the ETUC offers unusual promise. Again because of TUC initiative and leadership as a mediating force, many of the ideological impediments to collective action have been removed or reduced in importance. Though the CGT, the French Communist union, is still not a member of the ETUC because of the objections of the French Force Ouvrière, the Italian Communists have been admitted to membership and the CGT is informally consulted about ETUC policy. This would have been unthinkable even a few years ago, but its accomplishment greatly strengthens the claim of the ETUC to speak for European labour, which until 1969, twelve years after the Treaty of Rome, had no direct spokesman in the EEC.

It is, of course, not yet clear what the ETUC will achieve in terms of policy influence. Unemployment is the first important issue, though it can be said that the ETUC has handled well the more minor issues such as manpower training, health and safety questions, and the like. But whatever the future strength of the ETUC, the TUC is well placed to use its representations. The TUC exercises disproportionate influence in the ETUC at present largely because of its early role in founding the organization and then its continuous interest in helping to shape the direction of its policies ever since. This strength was confirmed again more recently when the TUC played an important role in replacing Theo Rasschaert as ETUC General Secretary with Mathias Hinterscheid, head of Luxembourg's trade union organization. Hinterscheid won TUC support largely because he is in favour of pressing for an aggressive ETUC interested in developing the most influential access possible to EEC institutions.

B. THE ECONOMIC AND SOCIAL COMMITTEE (ESC)

The ESC provides the most formal direct access for the TUC to the EEC. It is not, however, the most effective. The prominence of the ESC is due to its place in the Rome Treaty as the forum designated for the social partners, including unions, employers, farmers, and other interests, to be consulted. But in the words of one of its own officials, the ESC is "not exactly a pariah but neither is it a member of the Community's Gotha: it is rather more like the scholarship boy at Oxbridge in the old days, there less by right than of necessity."[6]

This description summarizes quite well the reasons for which the TUC finds the ESC less relevant to its purposes than other bodies.[7] From its foundation the ESC has been a consultative body and not a bargaining or conflictual forum. The experience of the TUC in Britain since the Second World War, after all, has been as a central actor in economic decision-making, with influence significant enough to determine at several points whether policy is implemented. By comparison the ESC is not in the mainstream of decision-making, nor even crucial in the channels of consultation. Worse still from the union point of view, its possible influence is seriously limited by the presence of ill-defined "other interests", while important EEC officials or national ministers are frequently absent from its meetings.

The organization of the ESC in summary is based on three groups of representatives. Group I is for employers, Group II for trade unionists, and Group III, equal in number to each of the others, is an amorphous collection of interests that run the gamut from farmers to craftsmen, from dealers to persons representing consumer organizations and even members of the general public without specific affiliation. The total membership is 144, with 24 members each for the large countries, 12 for Belgium and the Netherlands, nine for Denmark and Ireland, and six for Luxembourg. This entitles the TUC to nine seats on the Committee. These are filled, like the others, on the basis of nominations made by the British government; but in practice the names are put forward by the TUC General Council.

The composition and quality of representation in the Committee are from the unions' point of view unsatisfactory.[8] The TUC would clearly prefer that the ESC be composed entirely of producing interests, in particular of employers and unionists. They scorn Group III representatives as irrelevant to the interests of the other two groups. Moreover, they count Group III representatives as basically pro-business and therefore anti-labour – which they believe tilts the balance in the ESC against the unions.

If all of this were not bad enough, the TUC adds a further complaint that Group III representatives are poor in quality, though only slightly worse than employer representatives. They point to the frequent attendance of high-level union leaders. Yet, at the same time, employers often send junior executives, while Group III is populated with a number of retired persons whose only occupation is service on the ESC, more or less as a reward for past achievements rather than as spokespersons for particular groups.[9]

The work of the ESC: an assessment. The most important concern for the TUC is its assessment of the nature and influence of the ESC's work. The TUC's concern extends beyond outcomes in the Community to the effect ESC opinions have on member governments, given that they still exercise primary influence on the course of policies such as wages and working conditions which are of vital concern to unionists.

Historically, the major deficiency of the ESC has been its very weak role in Community decision-making.[10] The problem of representation has clearly reduced the possibility for the ESC to reach informed, coherent opinions on most issues. But worse, it has suffered from its place in a sort of no-man's land in the Community's law-making process. From the beginning of the Community, the ESC was designated as a purely consultative body, and consultation was quite restricted. Proposals originate with the Commission, are inevitably sent to the Council and in most cases to the Parliament. In practice, the ESC has been consulted far more frequently than the Treaty prescribes, because the Council and Commission have increasingly exercised their right to consult the ESC on any issue they consider appropriate. But consultation has usually occurred well after proposals have been worked out, and has largely involved technical and detailed issues. Historically the Council and Commission have rarely asked the ESC for its views on the broader economic and social issues. This pattern has had the further negative effect, from the TUC's perspective, of restricting the ESC to Community business to the exclusion of matters relating directly to national policies.

The most promising development for the ESC is its right since 1974 to consider and produce opinions on any subject affecting the Community. The Committee is now free to roam far and wide in

Community business and offer its opinions. But it has not overcome the problem that other institutions are still not bound to consider its opinions seriously. Therefore, though there is some potential, the ESC can hardly yet rank as comparable to Britain's National Economic Development Council. Thus, while the TUC finds the ESC useful because of its direct access and its new flexibility, it looks for alternative forums that can better re-create more familiar producer group politics.

C. SPECIALISED COMMITTEES, CONFERENCES, INFORMAL CONTACTS, AND OTHER CHANNELS OF ACCESS

Far more promising for the TUC as vehicles for access to Europe and the Community are the direct contact forums that proliferate each year. Their advantages are simply that they approach more closely the producer group relationships that occur in European domestic contexts. Specialized committees, *ad hoc* conferences and interpersonal communications are all included. The two most important so far on the unemployment issue are the Standing Committee on Employment and the Tripartite Economic and Social Conference.

1. The Standing Committee on Employment provides for consultation between trade unions, employers and the Council of Ministers for social affairs. The Committee meets about twice a year, taking up a variety of questions dealing with employment but usually with a fairly specific focus. Besides unemployment, typical issues include the illegal migration of labour, equality between men and women workers, the use of the European Social Fund in support of labour interests and a myriad of other specific and technical questions. The discussions usually focus on proposals submitted by the Commission, though more recently union representatives have broadened their scope.

It is important to note that union representation on the Committee is based on the European-level organizations, of which the ETUC is the largest. TUC leaders sit on the Committee but as representatives of the ETUC rather than of the British unions. The effect of this form of representation is to emphasize European unionism as a form of expression while still providing for national representation. The TUC's stake in the ETUC's development has obviously been strengthened by the growing importance of such specialized committees. In this forum, therefore, the best prospects for advancing TUC interests rest with creating a forceful ETUC. As yet the Committee is still a talking-shop and not a decision-making body. However, its contacts and format are far more likely to yield influence by conveying views and defining objectives than is possible through the ESC.

2. The Tripartite Economic and Social Conference is a newer body with representation similar to the Standing Committee on Employment. Its first meeting was held in November 1975, the second during June 1976, and then a year later in June 1977. Largely the creation of the ETUC, the Conference is a forum for the broadest range of economic and social questions. Since there have been at this point only three meetings it is difficult to gauge how effective the Conference will become. Its strength is that it brings together trade unionists and employers with both EEC Commissioners and finance and labour ministers to discuss the important issues that would not otherwise be debated within the Community. The potential importance of the Conference is certainly not as an action body, since it has no permanent staff and meets for only one day at a time. However, it can serve usefully as a place of dialogue and more importantly as a stimulant for actions or organizational innovation elsewhere, primarily within the context of the Community's institutions.

3. Besides the Tripartite Conference and the Standing Committee on Employment there are a number of other advisory committees in the EEC on which the TUC has direct representation. These include committees on the European Social Fund, Free Movement of Workers, Social Security for Migrant Workers, Vocational Training and Safety, and Hygiene and Health Protection. In the main these committees, except the Social Fund Committee, tend to work in narrow areas. It is interesting to note, though, that unions have generally been particularly influential in these more technical areas where their expertise is respected and required.

4. In addition, a great many other committees convened by the Commission involve trade unions, not by national federations, but with reference to particular industries. For example, there is the Consultative Committee of the European Coal and Steel Community including union leaders on the same basis as the ESC. Nominations are made in practice from specific industry committees such as, in the case of Britain, the Steel Industry Trade Union Consultative Committee. Though the TUC is informed of

selections, it takes no active part in the nomination procedure or the work of the committees.

5. Finally, the TUC can contact directly or through the ETUC Commissioners or EEC civil servants. Werner Feld points out that although the Commissioners individually seem to be 'quite elusive', contacts with middle and upper-rank Commission officials appear to be more fruitful.[11] "Through them it is often possible to obtain advance information on proposals planned by the Commission and to disseminate information memos that might serve to influence individuals who were doing the 'pick and shovel' preparation for the elaboration of Commission proposals."[12] Feld's comments are especially relevant to the extent that the civil servants are recruited from the ranks of the group seeking to influence it. Several former TUC employees, for example, can be found now working either in the Brussels or the London office of the EEC on labour questions. Such individuals seem to provide the TUC with important access points for informational as well as bargaining purposes.

The strategic importance of this relationship is illustrated in part by the TUC's concern that Britain has not so far obtained its just share of civil service positions in the EEC bureaucracy. This relationship, which is now only in its early stages, is different from that which British unions have with British civil servants. In the national context, civil servants usually develop their relationships with the union federation as part of their work experience and not as part of any previous relationships. In the EEC there has been an interest in recruiting officials who arrive with expertise and contacts. It is important to add, however, that EEC civil servants with previous trade union ties are not union "plants" sent over to the EEC on loan or with the express purposes of representing union interests *per se*. Often they are former union officials who have simply moved to what they saw as a better job opportunity, bringing with them an inevitable carry-over of contacts and attitudes that provide fruitful openings for the TUC in its efforts to influence the EEC.

III THE TUC'S INITIATIVE ON UNEMPLOYMENT: SOME SUCCESS AND MUCH FRUSTRATION

A. PRELUDE

During the middle months of 1975 a number of new elements came together to produce the initiative on unemployment in Europe. The referendum, of course, ended the long debate over British membership in the EEC and allowed the TUC to take up its seats on several committees and to carry its traditional function of protecting working people into the wider European context. At the same time the British recession pushed unemployment levels up rapidly and the TUC began to recognize more fully than ever before that it would not be able simply to dictate reflation.

The beginning of the transition in TUC perceptions seems to have occurred during April. A little over a month earlier the TUC had published its annual *Economic Review*. Unemployment had already risen from 653,000 in November 1974 to just over 770,000; and taking note of this rise and grim prospects to come, the *Economic Review* encouraged the government to invoke the classic remedy of higher public expenditures.[13] It was with great surprise therefore that the TUC learned during April that not only was the Chancellor, Dennis Healey, not going to take their advice, but that he would respond to the recession by cutting expenditure by about £1 billion in the coming year. Further, the only remedy that Healey offered to soothe the TUC was a batch of selective palliatives that would soften but certainly not solve or even greatly relieve the problems of recession. The General Council's public reaction was angry but noticeably laced with resignation. The budget, they said, " . . . would disappoint trade unionists in that it did nothing to prevent the emergence of higher unemployment towards the end of 1975."[14] But the General Council took no action and made no threats.

The wage restraint agreement of July 1975 followed almost the same pattern but showed even more strongly that the TUC recognized the economic and political constraints on its freedom of action. While the TUC–Labour Party Liaison Committee spoke bravely of targets to reduce unemployment, the major business of the negotiations between the Labour Government and the unions was the TUC's acceptance of very hard times to come, with high unemployment and probably a significant fall in the standard of living. It seems to have been at that moment, during July, that union leaders and especially Len Murray, the TUC General Secretary, began to consider the European initiative as an alternative to their shrinking domestic options.

The TUC's European strategy emerged over the following six months but it would be wrong to give the impression that it was a

well-planned or precise exercise. Rather, the TUC lurched forward
much in the way it works domestically, pressing in new directions as
its leaders saw them open, pushed on by each month's worsening
figures on unemployment and the economy.

The TUC took advantage of two openings into Europe. The first
was simply its physical move to take its seats in the EEC institutions
that it had boycotted since 1973. The second was the exercise of
active leadership in the long effort by the ETUC to press the
unemployment issue and the consequences of recession within the
EEC generally.

B. SOME SUCCESS, 1975–76

1. *Through the ETUC*

The TUC had been involved in a minor, unadvertised fashion with
the ETUC campaign on unemployment since the beginning of
1975. At the outset and until mid-year, the TUC hoped that the
ETUC efforts would boost, in however small a way, its own interest
in encouraging the British Government to reflate the domestic
economy, with special attention to maintaining or improving
employment levels. It was in this vein that during February 1975
the General Council prevailed on the ETUC Executive Committee
to issue a statement calling on governments to take joint action to
maintain economic activity and standards of living and to sustain
demand in order to tackle the problem of unemployment.

Later, with the referendum over, the TUC began to assert its
leadership over the direction of the ETUC initiative. Its influence
seems to be clear from July onwards. One month earlier the ETUC
Executive Committee had staged a conference on unemployment
which had "reviewed measures taken in Western European
countries and the policies of affiliated organizations to safeguard
employment and to protect living standards."[15] The specific
suggestions that flowed from that meeting were micro-economic in
nature, and primarily about training, unemployment benefits and
many of the selective measures that the TUC had discussed with the
British government.

While the TUC certainly supported this internationalization of
selective measures, its interest in Europe was more concerned with
winning the macro-economic policies that it could not get at home.
The July meeting of the ETUC Executive Committee reviewed the
work of the June conference and, taking its cues from the British

attitude, strongly criticized the scope of the conference's recommendations. For example, the Executive Committee pointed out that the ETUC should be working to encourage a new relationship with the raw-material-producing countries which would lead to agreements ensuring steady supplies of raw materials at relatively stable prices over a long period of time.[16] In addition, the Committee stressed that not every West European country was in the same situation and that consequently no single set of measures would be appropriate to all – a long-standing British theme. The Committee even went so far, under British prodding, as to insist that it incorporate its criticisms and suggestions in a new version of that report, and that it proceed from there to press the whole batch of recommendations on the European Community and the European Free Trade Association.

In November 1975 the first Tripartite Economic and Social Conference was held. The mere holding of the meeting was a victory because it brought together for the first time the unions, employers, EEC Commissioners and finance and labour ministers in a dialogue about broad economic policy, in this case specifically about the problem of unemployment. About 100 people participated, including two Commissioners, two officials from the Council Secretariat, 19 government ministers, 32 representatives for employers' organizations and 33 trade unionists (from four organizations) of whom 29 represented the ETUC. From a substantive point of view, though, the Conference was a disappointment, partly due to inadequate preparation. The failure to prescribe in advance any mechanism for reaching agreements was particularly unfortunate. The ETUC did offer a working paper analysing the causes of the recession and offering remedies, but the Commission, employers, and government ministers failed to respond in any coherent way. The only decision possible then was a decision to hold further conferences in the future.

The General Council of the TUC was highly critical of the November meeting, as were nearly all the participants. There was obvious satisfaction that the meeting had finally taken place and that it offered promise as a forum for future dialogue, but the General Council complained that better preparations could have yielded substantial decisions instead of none at all. The next meeting was scheduled for June 1976 and the General Council urged that the ETUC prepare a more dynamic report including suggestions for precise target setting and mechanisms for reviewing policy implementation. In addition, "a representative of the General Council pointed out that [in November] no account had been laid before the Conference of measures taken in the Community countries, nor any appraisal of their effect, and drew attention to the need for Community countries with balance of payments surpluses to take measures and concerted action, and for governments to consider the use of selective import controls when particular industries were seriously threatened as a result of overseas competition."[17]

The Second Conference by contrast was far more productive and significant. Preparations took a full four months and led to important agreement among all the participants at the one-day session in June. Following the suggestions of all the participants, including the ETUC, the Commission initiated a pre-conference dialogue. In March, the Commission issued a draft document which "set out its ideas on the origins of the present economic crisis and the lessons to be drawn from it, and put forward possible ways of overcoming it."[18] This document then became the subject of extensive consultations: the ETUC reacted in detail. At the end of May, the Commission issued a second, revised document which then – with modifications – became the basis for the final agreement.

These pre-conference negotiations from the Commission's document to the final statement of agreement at the end of the Conference were important steps forward. The Conference had at least become an accepted forum for trade union participation. Government ministers in particular had concluded after the first meeting that the Conference had been no more than a public relations ploy for the unions. They had agreed to a second meeting largely as a matter of courtesy without expecting improvement. The dialogue and the eventual agreement proved however, to be quite useful. Though the Conference was still very short, it served well as a focus for clarifying some policy goals. Most importantly though, the decisions taken at the Conference represented the first substantial influence of trade unionists on broad economic policy in a European context.

The major substantive gain of the Second Conference was target setting. This has been a primary goal of TUC recommendations both at home and to the ETUC and the Conference. Full employment should be achieved by 1980, the Conference agreed, and by 1978 the cyclical component of unemployment should be eliminated.[19] To accomplish these goals, the annual rate of growth until 1980 would have to be about 5 per cent, with the rate of inflation brought down by 1980 to 4–5 per cent a year.

The other area in which the TUC and the ETUC were especially successful was in winning a commitment to undertake constant review of the progress toward these goals. Both had suggested that the Standing Committee on Employment should undertake this function: "The TUC share the view of the ETUC that the Standing Committee on Employment should be entrusted with the task of monitoring progress in achieving the targets set. Its composition and terms of reference will need to be modified – we would want the finance ministers to take a full part since principal power and responsibility in this field lies with them."[20] The Conference statement did not go so far, but it did authorize the Standing Committee on Employment to pay "particular attention to the specific measures designed to help improve the situation".[21] More importantly though, it added that " . . . the Economic Policy Committee will, moreover, establish contact with the representatives of employers and labour for the purpose of periodically examining with them short-term economic prospects and the Community's medium term programme."[22] Thus a new avenue of approach and participation has emerged for trade unionists through the Economic Policy Committee, which may usefully supplement the periodic Tripartite Conferences.

But it must be stressed that the unions certainly did not come away with all or perhaps even most of what they had wanted. They did not win, for example, commitments on whole sets of specific and selective measures, such as an attempt to persuade Japan to reduce its exports to the Community, or the search for long-term raw materials agreements with developing nations, or the wider use of the Regional and Social Funds and the European Investment Bank, to relieve the unemployment problem. Nor did they learn how the member governments or the Community intended to achieve the agreed targets; and the TUC failed to gain acceptance for its proposal that the better-off countries should lead recovery by deliberate reflation.

2. Through the Economic and Social Committee

The strategy and tactics of the TUC initiative in Europe are in some ways more visible in the work of the ESC, simply because the TUC is represented there in its own right, whereas representation in the Standing Committee on Employment or the Tripartite Conference is through the ETUC. Since the TUC can press its own views directly through initiatives in the ESC, it can use favourable outcomes to increase pressure on the British government to support its proposals in other European institutions, especially in the Council of Ministers. This is particularly important on issues that are 'British' and therefore lack sufficient European appeal to generate ETUC support. For example, the British government might well have a strong interest in pressing the TUC's favourite theme that the better-off countries ought to lead a general European recovery through domestic reflation. This argument is more controversial in the ETUC where German unions, while sympathetic to British problems, are generally cooler to the idea because of their preoccupation with the threat of inflation.

Since taking its seats on the ESC in September 1975 the TUC has operated very much with these possibilities in mind. While it pressed the unemployment issue first through the ETUC, it also pressed just as hard through the ESC and at home through the British government to the Council of Ministers.

The failure of the First Tripartite Conference in November 1975 provided an incentive for the TUC to explore the possibilities of the ESC. The number of unemployed in December 1975 was 50 per cent higher than in June. Jack Jones and David Basnett led the pressure within the General Council for action.[23] As leaders of recession-hit public-sector unions, both were naturally very disturbed. They were also well placed to influence their colleagues because both were members of the TUC's Economic Policy and International Committees as well as the ESC. Together with Len Murray, the TUC's General Secretary, and also a member of the ESC, Jones and Basnett were most influential in the whole ESC initiative.[24]

The first stage in the TUC's approach to the ESC came at its January meeting.[25] Only a few days before the meeting, Len Murray asked the ESC Secretariat to put the unemployment issue on that month's agenda as an urgent matter. His request was highly irregular because the normal ESC procedure is not to deal with questions in plenary session until they have been considered by one of its specialized sections, which in this case would have been the Section for Economic and Financial Questions. After some discussion, the Secretariat refused to allow a formal debate leading to an opinion, but they did agree to Murray presenting a statement on the issue.

Murray's statement reviewed the problem of unemployment.[26] He urged, again as a matter of urgency, that the Section for Economic and Financial Questions prepare very quickly a draft opinion to be considered at the February meeting of the full Committee. This was yet another unusual request for the relatively slow-moving ESC but Murray prevailed (after some behind-the-scenes arm-twisting) and with only five days' notice the Section took up the issue during the following week.

The Section asked David Basnett to write the draft opinion based on a TUC paper. This " . . . called on governments to come together at Community level to coordinate their economic policies so as to achieve mutually consistent employment, growth, and balance of payments targets within a specified time."[27] It also urged national governments to insist on advance notice of layoffs, and called for temporary employment subsidies, regional subsidies, expansion of construction industries, financial help to build up stocks, to promote investments, and to undertake public works projects. While recognizing the limited scope for the Community to take substantive steps, it requested the use of the Regional and Social Funds and the European Investment Bank to help the unemployment problem. Finally, it urged that "within the Community a special responsibility falls on those countries with balance of payments surpluses to take a lead in expanding their level of demand whether for investment or otherwise."[28]

The ESC at its February meeting then accepted the draft opinion in almost its entirety by a vote of 40 votes to three with 14 abstentions. Employers unsuccessfully suggested a number of amendments, in the main stressing the need to control inflation, or asking that references to employment subsidies, regional assistance and the build-up of stocks be removed. The TUC thus emerged with nearly all of its suggestions intact, and the ESC opinion resembled very much the menu of suggestions that the TUC had been pushing in the ETUC and in the Tripartite Conference with less success.

The TUC took its victory in the form of the ESC draft opinion straight back to the British government. Its leaders met in the last days of February 1976 with James Callaghan, then Foreign Secretary and as such responsible for EEC affairs. It was not difficult in that meeting for the TUC leaders to win Callaghan's promise to carry the ESC opinion forward. The Government, after all, was also interested in finding solutions to the unemployment problem in a

European or Community context.[29] Furthermore, the Government
was anxious to assuage the bruised feelings of the union movement
that were hurting union-Labour relations.

Callaghan kept his promise in March at the Foreign Minister's
meeting. He led a discussion about unemployment and in the end
persuaded his colleagues to agree to put the matter on the agenda
for the forthcoming Heads-of-State meeting. Prime Minister Wilson, however, achieved rather less as his long speech on unemployment to the April summit failed to stir any real interest. The TUC
then shifted its attention back to the ETUC and the preparations for
the Tripartite Conference in June.

c. much frustration, 1976–78

The second Tripartite Conference in June 1976 proved to be the
high point of TUC satisfaction with its European initiative. Its
success at the Conference and earlier at the ESC rested on winning
commitments for action. Implementation was quite a different
matter, as was the development of continuing influence of the kind
that the TUC enjoyed in Britain. On these matters, TUC leaders
had learned nothing during their initiatives which suggested that
such influence or policy changes would be forthcoming any time
soon. Quite to the contrary, TUC leaders came away distinctly
worried that nothing would happen to give substance to the many
promises that they had heard. They concluded pessimistically, in
fact, that the web of committees, cumbersome procedures and the
sheer problem of consulting with the Community and so many
national governments would prove to be an insurmountable and
nearly permanent obstacle.

These concerns were the subject during August 1976 of a
searching General Council review of its European initiative.[30] The
Council at that time already had doubts that the recently concluded
Tripartite Conference would produce tangible gains in the fight
against unemployment. TUC leaders who had participated in the
European initiative were particularly cynical. They complained
that trade unionists simply lacked any leverage to compel governments to listen, let alone to accept their views. The structure of the
Community, they argued, gave unionists access primarily to the
Commission though it was the Council that took the major
decisions.

The General Council decided that day to make a concerted effort to improve its access and influence in the Community and with its member states by pressing for significant reform. It decided to strike out in a number of directions. These included an effort to convince the ETUC to intensify its work as well as to make its goals more explicit; to reform the Economic and Social Committee; and to remould the Standing Committee on Employment into a regular and influential consultative organization to the Council. Also, and most importantly, the General Council decided to press the British government to take a joint "British" approach in the Community. The Council said there should be "closer co-ordination between trade union organizations, employers and the Government in the United Kingdom on Community issues so that British interests might be defended and advanced."[31]

Two years later in the middle of 1978 the General Council could look back at these goals, harbouring the considerable frustration that it had accomplished none of them. Its worst fears about British membership in the Community had come true. Unemployment had risen from 4.85 million in the member countries at the time of the hopeful 1976 Tripartite Conference to more than 6 million by the middle of 1978. Moreover, in one effort after another in those two years the TUC had met failure in its attempt to reform European relationships.

The British government, for example, was a particularly disappointing ally in this respect. The Foreign and Commonwealth Office was perfectly willing to listen to TUC grumblings and willing continuously to remind Ministers to take TUC views "into account" on European matters. But it was not interested in developing a British "alliance" nor was it willing to support significant institutional reforms. It dismissed the possibility of throughgoing reform of the Economic and Social Committee as unfeasible because it would require changes in the Treaty of Rome. It lent only lukewarm and vague support to the possibility of changes in the Standing Committee on Employment. Most disappointing for the TUC, however, was the relative timidity of the British government in using its six months' presidency of the Council in the first half of 1977. The TUC thought that this period would be an especially favourable time to press for change but in the end the only applause it could offer for the presidency was for John Silkin's efforts to reform the Common Agricultural Policy.

The same disappointing results flowed from the TUC's more direct efforts at reform. It failed in the ESC to win more than a commitment to review the Committee's work with an eye to possible recommendations at some later point. The TUC's colleagues in the ETUC were sympathetic to the TUC's complaints and supported their demands but in general proved to be relatively weak and divided allies. The Standing Committee on Employment, in some contrast, did proceed to discuss specific issues such as work-sharing and the possibilities of increasing employment in the tertiary sector. But the TUC did not succeed in winning acceptance of its proposals for much more frequent meetings nor for representation by other ministers, especially those with financial and economic responsibilities.

The sum of the last two years has therefore been quite pessimistic. The main criticism of August 1976 – that the Council and the Community in general are not really accountable to the trade union movement – remains as valid for the TUC as ever before. Its suggestions at the Economic and Social Committee that representatives of the Council appear at its sessions and give an account of the impact of ESC opinions has so far fallen on deaf ears. And there is no sign of real change in the offing. Rather, the Tripartite Conference of June 1977, which acknowledged that the targets set the year before would not be met and failed to make new commitments or set new goals or consider new reforms, probably offered the best evidence of the frustration that the TUC has found in Europe.

CONCLUDING COMMENTS

The TUC turned to Europe because its influence in Britain was weakening and because the British government had not adopted the remedial policies for the recession demanded by the TUC's membership. The General Council also recognized the internationalization of economic policy-making and therefore its own stake in influencing a widening decision process.

The TUC's experience in Europe in the case of unemployment indicates that it depends for its influence on the active support of both European trade unionism and the British government. The problem, however, is that the effective support of each is uncertain. In the case of European trade unionism, the TUC has done a yeoman job in helping to overcome the historical divisiveness of ideology, but it has not been able so far to overcome the continuing pull of nationalism. Too many vital issues, including employment, wages, and working conditions, exacerbate differences in national priorities, precedents and sensitivities. This makes it difficult and on occasion impossible to organize ETUC strength in support of specific and detailed policies. The ETUC has conducted a vigorous, broadly-based campaign against unemployment. But differences such as those between the British and German unions over the question of German reflation have undermined these efforts, thus demonstrating the weaknesses of international trade unionism as compared to national trade unionism. There is little evidence that nationalism is declining; in fact, nationalism seems to be more disabling during recessions, at just the time when the effectiveness of the ETUC could be most useful.

The problems of making international trade unionism effective are all the more unfortunate for TUC interests because the best opportunities for influence seem to be offered through bodies that require ETUC representation. The Standing Committee on Employment in particular might become, if the unions have their way, a sort of on-going Tripartite Conference. Also, the Economic Policy Committee may become important for union interests. While TUC leaders participate in the Standing Committee, they do so as part of the ETUC delegation and are thus restrained from making these forums the focus of domestic-style collectivist politics.

The other TUC approach, on its own through the ESC, raises questions about British government support. Though the TUC was successful in the ESC, producing an opinion which was nearly a statement of its own views, the influence of that opinion on the Community and on other national governments depended on the willingness and ability of the British government to carry it forward. While the British government in that case took up the TUC view, subsequent experience showed that such support will not easily be forthcoming on other issues. Though British government support is not necessarily decisive for TUC efforts in Europe, it is an important adjunct to the TUC's other European initiatives.

The relevance of such support is enhanced to the extent that the British government is likely to be a natural and sympathetic spokesman for TUC goals because of a shared concern for British problems. Though growing economic interdependence causes the TUC to work for international economic policies, its basic concerns about employment, wages and working conditions are still rooted in a national context. The unemployment issue is a good example. The

British government has been more supportive of the TUC's recommendations than the ETUC. Its support in 1976, for example, was strong both because Labour demonstrated its loyalty to the union movement and because the international solution to unemployment on TUC terms, including German reflation, fitted neatly into the broad framework of British government policy.[32]

It is not hard to imagine, though, that government support for TUC goals and strategies in Europe in the future could become the subject of sharp bargaining. In that eventuality domestic political relationships will undoubtedly play a major role, just as they already have in a number of different ways. The familiar ties between Labour and the unions will certainly continue to be very important. By contrast however, the Conservatives' relationship with the trade union movement has been marked by mutual hostility, distrust and distance worsened by the 1974 events. The union movement puts a premium on conflict with the Conservatives, using it as a rallying-point for union solidarity. However, if government support in Europe becomes a valuable commodity, the TUC may find it worth while to work out a more cooperative relationship. Conversely, a Conservative Government (and to a lesser extent Labour Governments) may find in the TUC's work in Europe a certain leverage encouraging cooperation as a price for its support.

In conclusion, the TUC's problem so far has been that in Europe it has been forced to operate in an uncomfortably dependent role, needing the support of either the ETUC or the British government as its spokesman. The efforts of the ETUC are more attenuated and less aggressive than the domestic campaigns of the TUC in Britain. The problem with dependence on the British government is that its support carries costs, perhaps very steep costs with a Conservative government. Any government could take advantage of that dependence to put pressure on the TUC in a vulnerable situation. Such a situation developed into a new pattern of relationship would offer a tantalizing possibility for a "way out" of Britain's chronic economic paralysis.

Notes

CHAPTER 1

1. For some excellent insights into Britain's contemporary economic problems, see Samuel Brittan, *The Economic Consequences of Democracy* (Temple Smith, 1977). Also see the earlier book by Brittan, *Steering the Economy* (Secker & Warburg, 1969).
2. The first and most dramatically influential book criticizing the unions was by Michael Shanks, *The Stagnant Society* (Penguin, 1961).
3. The most influential work in proposing the terms of this agreement was by Sir William Beveridge, *Full Employment in a Free Society* (Allen & Unwin, 1944); earlier, see also Sir William Beveridge, *Social Insurance and Allied Services* (Macmillan, 1942).
4. The document which specifically defined the commitment to permanent full employment was Ministry of Reconstruction, *Employment Policy*, Cmd 6527.
5. John Maynard Keynes, *The General Theory of Employment, Interest, and Money* (Harcourt, Brace & World, 1936).
6. This view is drawn from the work of Professor Samuel Beer, who offered his important notion of collectivist politics in Britain in *Modern British Politics* (Faber, 1965).
7. See Gerald A. Dorfman, *Wage Politics in Britain 1945–1967* (Iowa State University Press, 1973, and Charles Knight, 1974); also see several other excellent books including: Leo Panitch, *Social Democracy and Industrial Militancy* (Cambridge University Press, 1976); and T. C. May, *Trade Unions and Pressure Group Politics* (Saxon House, 1975).
8. Gerald A. Dorfman, *Wage Politics in Britain*, chaps 5, 6.
9. Ibid., chap. 4.
10. Ibid., chap. 7.

CHAPTER 2

1. *Royal Commission on Trade Unions and Employers' Associations 1965–1968: Chairman, the Rt. Hon. Lord Donovan, Report* (HMSO, 1968) Cmnd 3623 (hereafter cited as the Donovan Report).
2. *Fair Deal at Work* (Conservative Political Centre, April 1968).
3. Gerald A. Dorfman, *Wage Politics in Britain*, chaps 5, 6.
4. Interview with George Woodcock, 26 July 1972.
5. *Donovan Report*, p. 12.

6. Ibid., p. 36.
7. Ibid., p. 262.
8. Ibid., p. 267.
9. Ibid.
10. Ibid., p. 262.
11. *Fair Deal at Work.*
12. Ibid., p. 12.
13. Ibid., p. 13.
14. Ibid., p. 15.
15. Ibid., pp. 15–16.
16. Ibid., p. 18.
17. Ibid.
18. Ibid., p. 19.
19. Ibid., p. 30.
20. Ibid.; including following points: B, C, D.
21. Ibid., pp. 31–67; including following points: 4, 5, 6.
22. Peter Jenkins, *The Battle of Downing Street*, (Charles Knight, 1970) p. 1.
23. Interview with Barbara Castle, 27 July 1972.
24. Unattributable interview.
25. Interview with Lord Greene, 24 July 1969.
26. Interview with James Mortimer, 5 August 1969.
27. Unattributable interview with member of the TUC staff, 10 July 1969.
28. Ibid.
29. For exposition of some of the discussion, but not all: TUC, *Annual Report 1968*, pp. 40–1.
30. Woodcock interview.
31. Castle interview.
32. Woodcock interview.
33. Ibid.
34. Jenkins, *The Battle of Downing Street*, p. 37.
35. Woodcock interview.
36. *In Place of Strife* (HMSO, 1969) Cmnd 3888.
37. Ibid., p. 1.
38. Castle interview.
39. *In Place of Strife*, p. 10.
40. Ibid., p. 13.
41. Interview with Frank Cousins, 5 August 1969.
42. Castle interview.
43. TUC, *Annual Report 1968*, pp. 570–2.
44. Ibid., p. 359.
45. Woodcock interview.
46. Jenkins, *The Battle of Downing Street*, pp. 37–9.
47. Woodcock interview; also, the TUC *Annual Report 1969* offers a less dramatic view of this meeting, pp. 126–7.
48. *The Guardian*, 3 January 1969; and Cousins interview.
49. TUC, *Annual Report 1969*, pp. 127–8.
50. *Guardian*, 3 January 1969; *Financial Times*, 15 January 1969.
51. *Financial Times*, 15 January 1969.
52. Interview with Reginald Prentice, July 1972.

53. *Financial Times*, 18 February 1969.
54. See especially the poll conducted by the Opinion Research Centre in *The Times*, 8 January 1969.
55. For example, see *Guardian*, 18 January 1969; *The Times* and *Financial Times*, 20 February 1969.
56. Unattributable interview.
57. *The Times*, 18 January 1969.
58. *Financial Times*, 18 January 1969.
59. At a meeting between Mrs Castle and the General Council on 21 January 1969. See TUC, *Annual Report 1969*, p. 131.
60. Ibid., pp. 131–2.
61. *Guardian*, 5 February 1969; and interview with AEW staff, 28 July 1972.
62. Unattributable interview with a member of the TGWU staff, 7 August 1972.
63. Interview with Hugh Gray, 8 July 1969.
64. The following examples were developed from an interview with Patrick Lowry, 8 August 1972.
65. Castle interview.
66. Unattributable interview.
67. *The Times*, 6 March 1969.
68. *The Times*, 27 March 1969.
69. Unattributable interview.
70. For a discussion of the Jenkins strategy, see *The Times*, 28 March 1969.
71. Unattributable interview.
72. Harold Wilson, *The Labour Government 1964–70* (Pelican Books, 1974) p. 805.
73. Unattributable interview with a member of the TUC Economic Committee.
74. TUC, *Annual Report 1969*, p. 132.
75. Ibid.
76. Eric Silver, *Victor Feather, TUC* (Gollancz, 1973) pp. 144–5.
77. Lord Greene interview.
78. *Financial Times*, 18 April 1969.
79. Ibid.
80. TUC, *Annual Report 1969*, p. 134.
81. TUC, *Programme for Action*, 1969.
82. Interview with Len Murray, 31 July 1969.
83. Silver, *Victor Feather, TUC*, pp. 146–7; and unattributable interview at Congress House.
84. Silver, *Victor Feather, TUC*, p. 148.
85. TUC, *Annual Report 1969*, p. 135.
86. Ibid.
87. Ibid.
88. Ibid., p. 136.
89. TUC, *Programme for Action*, p. 13.
90. Ibid.
91. *Guardian* and *Daily Mail*, 16 May 1969.
92. For a discussion of this important and explosive meeting, see TUC, *Annual Report 1969*, pp. 136–8; *Guardian*, *Financial Tmes* and *The Times*, 22 May 1969.
93. Lord Greene interview.
94. Silver, *Victor Feather, TUC*, p. 151; and unattributable interview with a member of the General Council.

95. Silver, *Victor Feather, TUC*, pp. 152–3; and Jenkins, *The Battle of Downing Street*, p. 140.
96. Silver, *Victor Feather, TUC*, p. 153.
97. Wilson, *The Labour Government 1964–70*, pp. 822–3.
98. Silver, *Victor Feather, TUC*, pp. 153–4.
99. TUC, *Programme for Action*, p. 23.
100. *The Times*, 9 June 1969.
101. Jenkins, *The Battle of Downing Street*, p. 139.
102. Lord Greene interview.
103. Murray interview.
104. TUC, *Annual Report 1969*, pp. 139–40; and *Guardian*, 10 June 1969.
105. See both Harold Wilson, *The Labour Government 1964–70*, p. 824; and Silver, *Victor Feather, TUC*, p. 156.
106. TUC, *Annual Report 1969*, pp. 140–1.
107. Ibid., p. 141.
108. Ibid.
109. Ibid., p. 142.
110. *The Times*, 12 June 1969; Lord Greene interview; and interview with John Torode, 23 August 1972.
111. TUC, *Annual Report 1969*, p. 143.
112. Ibid.
113. Castle interview.
114. Torode interview.
115. *The Times*, 13 June 1969.
116. Jenkins, *The Battle of Downing Street*, pp. 150–1.
117. Jenkins offers the best account of this period (*The Battle of Downing Street*, pp. 153–4) which this author has confirmed in several interviews. For contrast, see Harold Wilson's account in *The Labour Government 1964–70*, pp. 825–31.
118. Torode interview.
119. Wilson, *The Labour Government 1964–70*, p. 826.
120. Silver, *Victor Feather, TUC*, p. 158.
121. TUC, *Annual Report 1969*, pp. 144–5.
122. Interview with Lord Allen, 22 July 1969.
123. TUC, *Annual Report 1969*, p. 144.
124. Ibid.
125. Ibid.
126. Ibid., p. 145.
127. Lord Greene interview.
128. Silver, *Victor Feather, TUC*, p. 160.
129. TUC, *Annual Report 1969*, p. 145.
130. Silver, *Victor Feather, TUC*, pp. 160–1.
131. TUC, *Annual Report 1969*, p. 146.
132. *Daily Mail*, 20 June 1969; *The Economist*, 21 June 1969.

CHAPTER 3

1. *Fair Deal at Work* (Conservative Political Centre, April 1968).

2. *The Times*, 23 May 1970; and on numerous occasions during May and June 1970.

3. Gerald A. Dorfman, *Wage Politics in Britain*, chaps 5, 6.

4. *A Better Tomorrow* (Conservative Central Office, 1970).

5. This point and others about this strategy were expressed by a Conservative Parliamentary Private Secretary who wishes to remain anonymous, 2 August 1972.

6. Interviews with Lord Allen, 16 November 1974 and 10 August 1977; interviews with Lord Greene, 4 August 1972 and 31 July 1973.

7. For a summary of the recommendations discussed below, see *Fair Deal at Work*, pp. 61–7.

8. For examples, see Brian Weeks, Michael Mellish, Linda Dickens and John Lloyd, *Industrial Relations and the Limits of Law* (Blackwell, 1975); and A. W. J. Thomson and S. R. Englemenn, *The Industrial Relations Act* (Martin Robertson, 1975).

9. Industrial Relations Bill, *Consultative Document* (Department of Employment, 1970).

10. Lord Allen interview.

11. *Financial Times*, 14 October 1970.

12. Lord Greene interview.

13. Unattributable interview with members of TUC staff.

14. For precise description of TUC-led activities, see TUC, *Annual Report 1971*, pp. 96–8.

15. TUC, *Special Congress Report 1971*, pp. 48–9.

16. Ibid., pp. 54–7, 72–4.

17. Ibid., p. 63.

18. For example, see *The Times*, 2 November 1970, for stoppage at automobile component factory in Birmingham.

19. See Feather statement at Congress: TUC, *Special Congress Report 1971*, pp. 45–54 and especially p. 52.

20. Unattributable interview with every senior member of the General Council; Opinion Research Centre poll in *Evening Standard*, 9 November 1970.

21. Interview with Edward Heath, 13 April 1978.

22. For a full and perceptive discussion of the docks problem, see David F. Wilson, *Dockers* (Fontana/Collins, 1972).

23. For a legal description of the Heatons case, see Brian Weeks, *et al.*, *Industrial Relations and the Limits of Law*, pp. 106–10; for TUC account, see TUC, *Annual Report 1972*, pp. 89–92.

24. Newspaper accounts in the *Financial Times* and *Guardian* on 17 June 1972 describe this case. These descriptions were confirmed for this author in an interview with D. E. Hagen, Deputy Secretary of WIRC, 3 August 1972.

25. For an excellent review and analysis, see *Sunday Times*, 30 July 1972; also interview with Allen Brown, 21 July 1972.

26. Conservative Parliamentary Private Secretary who wishes to remain anonymous, 2 August 1972; and interview with Michael Shanks, 26 July 1972.

27. Interview with Michael Teague, 2 August 1972.

28. TUC, *Annual Report 1972*, pp. 104–5.

29. Lord Greene interview.

30. *Sunday Times*, 30 July 1972.

31. The author spent this day at the TUC and is reporting the mood first-hand.
32. Interview with Nicholas Scott, 26 July 1972.
33. *Guardian*, 28 July 1972.
34. Ibid.
35. Ibid.
36. *Sunday Times*, 30 July 1972.
37. *Guardian*, 28 July 1972.
38. *The Economist*, 22 April 1972, p. 11.
39. *The Economist*, 3 June 1972, p. 15.
40. Unattributable interview with Parliamentary Private Secretary.
41. For discussion about possible changes, see *Sunday Times*, 30 July 1972; for Maurice Macmillan's statement about the Government's attitude toward possible changes, see *The Times*, 2 August 1972; also personal interview with Macmillan, 16 August 1977.
42. For a discussion about the Industrial Charter, see Gerald Dorfman, *Wage Politics in Britain*, pp. 74–8.
43. *Department of Employment Gazette*, July 1973, pp. 621–2.
44. Ibid., p. 614.
45. Barber became Chancellor on July 26 after the sudden death of Iain MacLeod.
46. For the Chancellor's explanation of this policy to the TUC, see TUC, *Annual Report 1971*, pp. 246–7.
47. Ibid.
48. Lord Allen interview.
49. TUC, *Annual Report 1971*, pp. 246–7.
50. Interview with C. H. Urwin, 2 August 1977.
51. *Department of Employment Gazette*, July 1973, p. 612.
52. Silver, *Victor Feather, TUC*, p. 196; Jock Bruce-Gardyne, *Whatever Happened to the Quiet Revolution?* (Charles Knight, 1974) pp. 28–9; TUC, *Annual Report 1971*, pp. 45–6.
53. TUC, *Annual Report 1970*, p. 46; Bruce-Gardyne, *Whatever Happened to the Quiet Revolution?*, p. 29; Silver, *Victor Feather, TUC*, pp. 196–7.
54. Silver, *Victor Feather, TUC*, p. 197.
55. *Department of Employment Gazette*, July 1973, p. 632.
56. Ibid., p. 612.
57. TUC, *Economic Review 1970*.
58. For example, see the TUC meeting with Heath of 11 March 1971: TUC, *Annual Report 1971*, pp. 250–1.
59. Ibid.
60. Ibid., p. 251.
61. Unattributable interview with a member of the TUC staff.
62. Interview with George Woodcock, 26 July 1972, confirmed these concerns which Woodcock himself had earlier preached.
63. TUC, *Annual Report 1971*, pp. 254–9.
64. Ibid., p. 259.
65. Ibid., p. 260. It is interesting as well as significant that the TUC published a detailed review of the Chancellor's statement.
66. Ibid.
67. Ibid.
68. Ibid.

69. Ibid.
70. Ibid., p. 524.
71. Lord Greene interview.
72. John Hughes and Roy Moore (eds) provide a detailed account of the dispute from the NUM point of view in *A Special Case?* (Penguin, 1972); also see TUC, *Annual Report 1972*, pp. 97–9.
73. Ibid.
74. Ibid.,pp. 123–44.
75. For a full discussion of the rail dispute, see TUC, *Annual Report 1972*, pp. 100–3.
76. Silver, *Victor Feather, TUC*, p. 206.
77. Unattributable interview with a member of the General Council.
78. Ibid.
79. Silver emphasizes Feather's seriousness in the talks. But this author was told in mid-summer 1972 by a leading TUC negotiator who wishes to remain anonymous that the talks would fail. See Silver, *Victor Feather, TUC*, pp. 208–10.
80. Moderates provided the press with most of the information about union attitudes towards the talks, and they generally sounded optimistic.
81. Feather's own interest in agreement tended to blur the Prime Minister's view because Heath got most of his information from Feather.
82. Macmillan interview.
83. See Composite Motion 12, TUC, *Annual Report 1972*, pp. 554–5.
84. Unattributable interview with a senior member of the General Council.
85. TUC, *The Chequers and Downing Street Talks* (1972) pp. 3–4.
86. Ibid., pp. 5–7.
87. Ibid., p. 6.
88. *Sunday Times*, 5 November 1972.
89. *Silver, Victor Feather, TUC*, p. 210.
90. Heath interview.
91. Heath got on very well with Feather and trusted him: Heath interview.
92. Ibid.
93. See for example, *The Economist*, 7 October 1972.
94. TUC, *Chequers and Downing Street Talks*, pp. 14–18.
95. Ibid., pp. 15–16.
96. Ibid., p. 16.
97. Ibid., pp. 16–18.
98. Ibid., p. 17.
99. Ibid., p. 18.
100. Ibid., p. 19.
101. Ibid., pp. 19–21.
102. *The Times*, 3 November 1972.
103. Heath interview.
104. *The Times*, 12 January 1973.
105. TUC, *Annual Report 1973*, p. 278.
106. Ibid.
107. *Department of Employment Gazette*, July 1973, pp. 628–31.
108. TUC, *Annual Report 1973*, p. 281.
109. Ibid.; also n.104.
110. Lord Greene interview.

111. TUC, *Economic Policy and Collective Bargaining in 1973, Report of Special Trades Union Congress.*
112. Ibid., p. 53.
113. Ibid., pp. 98, 110.
114. Ibid., p. 86.
115. For example, see Feather's speech at the Special Congress, Ibid., pp. 54–61.
116. These secret talks were revealed in *The Times*, 3 May 1973.
117. Ibid.
118. *The Times*, 17 May and 24 May, 1973.
119. Ibid., 4 April 1973.
120. Lord Greene and Woodcock interviews. Though retired, Woodcock kept up contact with union leaders who sought his advice from time to time.
121. Ibid.
122. *The Times*, 24 May 1973.
123. Ibid.
124. Lord Greene and Woodcock interviews.
125. Interview with Alan Swindon, 17 August 1972.
126. Unattributable interview with Parliamentary Private Secretary.
127. Heath interview.
128. Ibid.
129. Stephen Fay and Hugo Young, "The Fall of Heath", *Sunday Times*, 1976
130. Ibid., p. 8.
131. Ibid., p. 7.
132. See n.76.
133. Fay and Young, *Fall of Heath*, p. 7.
134. Ibid.
135. Ibid.
136. Macmillan said that neither he nor his colleagues realized that the miners had slipped so badly in pay comparability over the two years since the 1972 settlement: Macmillan interview.
137. Fay and Young, *Fall of Heath*, p. 13.
138. *The Guardian*, 9 October 1973.
139. Fay and Young, *Fall of Heath*, p. 14.
140. Heath interview.
141. Interview with James Douglas, August 1976.
142. Fay and Young, *Fall of Heath*, p. 18.
143. *The Times*, 21 December 1973.
144. Fay and Young, *Fall of Heath*, p. 19.
145. Unattributable interview with member of the TUC staff.
146. Heath interview.
147. The author has confirmed this view during a number of interviews, including those with Lord Greene, Lord Allen, and C. H. Urwin.
148. Ibid.
149. TUC, *Annual Report 1974*, p. 22.
150. TUC, *The TUC's Initiatives*, p. 6.
151. Lord Allen interview.
152. *The Times*, 10 January 1974.
153. Fay and Young, *Fall of Heath*, p. 20.
154. TUC, *The TUC's Initiatives*, pp. 7–8.

155. Lord Allen, Lord Greene, and C. H. Urwin interviews.
156. TUC, *The TUC's Initiatives*, p. 9.
157. *The Times*, 16 January 1974.
158. Heath interview.
159. Ibid.
160. Ibid.
161. Ibid.
162. Ibid.
163. TUC, *The TUC's Initiatives*, pp. 9–10.
164. *The Times*, 22 January 1974.
165. TUC, *The TUC's Initiatives*, p. 10.
166. Fay and Young, *Fall of Heath*, pp. 21–2.
167. TUC, *Annual Report 1974*, p. 221.
168. *The Times*, 30 January 1974.
169. TUC, *The TUC's Initiatives*, p. 12.
170. *The Times*, 30 January 1974.
171. Urwin interview.
172. *The Times*, 29 January 1974.
173. Ibid.
174. Unattributable interviews with several trade union leaders.
175. Fay and Young, *Fall of Heath*, p. 29.
176. Ibid.

CHAPTER 4

1. TUC, *Annual Report 1971*, p. 98.
2. Gerald A. Dorfman, *Wage Politics in Britain*, pp. 31–2.
3. Ibid., p. 31.
4. Ibid., p. 32.
5. Interview with C. H. Urwin, 2 August 1977.
6. TUC, *Annual Report 1972*, pp. 105–8.
7. TUC – Labour Party Liaison Committee, *Economic Policy and he Cost of Living* (February 1973).
8. *Department of Employment Gazette*, June 1973, pp. 622, 628.
9. TUC *Annual Report 1973*, p. 312.
10. Ibid., p. 313.
11. Ibid.
12. Ibid., pp. 312–14.
13. TUC – Labour Party Liaison Committee, *Joint Statement on Social and Economic Policy* (1973).
14. Urwin interview.
15. This attitude was particularly noticeable in *The Economist*. Perusal of *The Economist* issues from late 1974 through mid- 1975 will demonstrate this point.
16. TUC, *Annual Report 1974*, pp. 395–8.
17. *Guardian, TUC Brighton*, 1974, p. 19.
18. Ibid.
19. TUC, *Annual Report 1974*, p. 289; TUC, *Collective Bargaining and the Social Contract* (1974) p. 5.

20. Unattributable interview with TUC staff member, 18 November 1974.
21. Interview with Lord Allen, 16 November 1974.
22. For a good discussion of this period of wage explosion, see Kevin Hawkins, *British Industrial Relations 1945–1975*, (Barrie & Jenkins, 1976).
23. Ibid., p. 160.
24. Urwin interview.
25. TUC, *Annual Report 1975*, pp. 264–73.
26. See issues of TUC's monthly *Labour* for the period from the fall of 1974 through the spring of 1975.
27. *Department of Employment Gazette*, July 1975, p. 700.
28. *The Times*, 11 August 1975.
29. I gained this impression first-hand while I did research at Congress House that summer.
30. Interview with George Foggon, 12 August 1975.
31. Interview with Donald Derx, July 1977.
32. Urwin interview.
33. Unattributable interview with a member of the TUC staff.
34. Interview with James Mortimer, 19 July 1977.
35. Interview with Lord Allen, 10 August 1977; Urwin interview.
36. Ibid.
37. TUC, *Annual Report 1975*, p. 272.
38. Ibid.
39. Ibid.
40. Ibid.
41. Interview with Alan Swindon, 17 August 1977.
42. TUC, *The Development of the Social Contract*, 1975.
43. *The Attack on Inflation* (HMSO, 1975) Cmnd 6151.
44. Ibid., pp. 13–14.
45. TUC, *Annual Report 1975*, pp. 455–80.
46. Ibid., p. 480.
47. Ibid., p. 456.
48. Ibid.
49. Ibid., p. 457.
50. For a detailed description of this process see TUC, *Annual Report 1976*, pp. 299–312.
51. *Department of Employment Gazette*, July 1976, p. 786.
52. TUC, *Annual Report 1976*, pp. 300–1.
53. Ibid., pp. 301–2.
54. TUC, *Economic Review 1976*.
55. Unattributable interview with a very senior member of the General Council.
56. *The Economist*, 17 April 1976, p. 75; 1 May 1976, pp. 11–13; and 8 May 1976, pp. 78–80.
57. TUC, *Special Congress Report 1976*, pp. 28–9.
58. TUC, *Annual Report 1976*, pp. 309–10.
59. Ibid., pp. 310–12.
60. Ibid.; see especially the speech by G. A. Drain, pp. 534–7.
61. Ibid., p. 309.
62. Ibid., pp. 309–10; and unattributable interview with a member of the General Council.

63. Ibid., pp. 310–12.
64. Ibid., p. 311.
65. Ibid., p. 312.
66. See various speeches at Congress: TUC, *Annual Report 1976*, pp. 518–29; 538–41.
67. Ibid., pp. 534–7.
68. Ibid., p. 521.
69. Ibid., pp. 526–8.
70. Ibid., pp. 528–9.
71. *The Times*, 8 October 1976.
72. Ibid.
73. Ibid, 11 October 1976; 12 October 1976; *Guardian*, 8 October 1976.
74. *The Times*, 27 October 1976; and unattributable interview with a member of the TUC staff.
75. *The Times*, 30 November 1976.
76. TUC, *Annual Report 1977*, p. 219.
77. *Guardian Weekly*, 2 January 1977.
78. Ibid.
79. *Department of Employment Gazette*, July 1977, p. 758.
80. Urwin interview.
81. Mortimer interview.
82. *Guardian Weekly*, 16 January 1977.
83. TUC, *Economic Review 1977*; a good summary can be found in TUC, *Annual Report 1977*, pp. 220–3.
84. *The Guardian*, 3 April 1977; and TUC, *Annual Report 1977*, p. 224.
85. Unattributable interview with a senior member of the General Council.
86. *The Attack on Inflation After 31st July 1977* (HMSO, 1977) Cmnd 6882.
87. Prices by early 1978 had fallen to an annual rate of increase of less than 10 per cent. See the *Department of Employment Gazette*, April 1978, p. 1978.
88. For a review of this period see the following articles: *The Times*, 8 December 1977, 17 January 1978, 17 April 1978; *The Economist*, 13 May 1978, 20 May 1978.

CHAPTER 5

1. For a definition and discussion of collectivist paralysis or, as it is sometimes styled, "pluralistic stagnation", see Samuel Beer, 'The British Legislature and the Problems of Mobilizing Consent', in *Lawmakers in a Changing World*, Elke Frank (ed.), p. 38.
2. TUC, *Economic Review 1976*, pp. 15–25.
3. Robert Lieber makes the same point in discussing an earlier period. See *British Politics and European Unity*, University of California Press (Berkeley), p. 40.
4. I conducted a number of non-attributable interviews on this topic with TUC officials and union leaders during the summers of 1975 and 1976 in London.
5. See especially TUC, *General Council's Report 1976*, pp. 232–4, 240–2, 313–14; also T. Parry, *Speech to Tripartite Economic and Social Conference*, 24 June 1976, mimeographed.

6. Diarmid McLaughlin, "The Work and Aims of the Economic and Social Committee", *Journal of Common Market Studies*, vol. xv, no. 1 (September 1976) pp. 9–28.

7. The views of General Council members about the relative shortcomings of EEC institutions, and especially the ESC, are to be found in a capsule from in *General Council's Report 1976*, p. 232.

8. Ibid.; *The Economist*, 6 March 1976, p. 63; and an unattributable interview, TUC, London, 23 July 1976.

9. Unattributable interviews, TUC and union offices, London, 6 August 1976.

10. The following assessment of the ESC's work is based primarily on Diarmid McLaughlin, op. cit.

11. Werner J. Feld, *The European Community in World Affairs*, (Knopf, 1976) p. 46.

12. Ibid.

13. TUC, *Annual Report 1975*, pp. 264, 266.

14. Ibid., p. 268.

15. TUC, *Annual Report 1975*, p. 217.

16. Ibid., p. 218.

17. TUC, *General Council's Report 1976*, p. 241.

18. Commission of the European Communities, *Restoring Full Employment and Stability in the Community*, Brussels, 26 May 1976, p. 1.

19. The full statement issued by the Conference is "Joint Statement by the Conference – on the restoration of full employment and stability in the Community", press release by the Council of the European Communities, Luxembourg, 24 June 1976 (754/76–Presse 70).

20. T. Parry, speech, p. 9.

21. *Joint Statement by the Conference* . . . p. 4.

22. Ibid.

23. Unattributable interview, union leader, London, 6 August 1976.

24. Ibid.

25. A brief summary of the TUC initiative in the ESC can be found in TUC, *General Council's Report 1976*, pp. 233–4.

26. "Statement Given by Mr. Murray", TUC, January 1976, mimeograph.

27. TUC, *General Council's Report 1976*, p. 233.

28. Economic and Social Committee, *Opinion of the Economic and Social Committee on Unemployment in the Community*, Brussels, 26 February 1976, p. 4.

29. TUC, *General Council's Report 1976*, p. 234.

30. TUC, *General Council's Report 1976*, pp. 168–70.

31. Ibid., p. 169.

32. "Callaghan Call for Joint Bid by Europe to Cut Jobless", *The Times*, 9 August 1976, p. 1.

Personal Interviews

Abbott, Janet, former Assistant to Alan Swindon, Director, Industrial Relations, Confederation of British Industry, 13 August 1975.

Allen, Lord, General Secretary, Union of Shop, Distributive, and Allied Workers; Chairman, TUC Economic Committee; member, TUC General Council: 22 July 1969, 16 November 1975, 10 August 1977.

Bendelow, Martin, Centre for Policy Studies, 22 July 1977.

Brown, Alan, Assistant Secretary, Department of Employment, 21 July 1972.

Butler, Michael, Assistant Under-Secretary in charge of European Community Affairs, 24 July 1975.

Carlton, Ann, Political Adviser, Ministry of Agriculture, 15 August 1977.

Castle, Barbara, former Secretary for Employment and Prices, 27 July 1972, 13–15 April 1978.

Coldrick, Peter, Secretary, European Trade Union Confederation, 29 July 1977 (by phone).

Cousins, Frank, General Secretary, Transport and General Workers Union; member, TUC General Council, 5 August 1969.

Derx, Donald, Deputy Secretary, Department of Employment, July, 1977.

Donovan, Lord (Terence Norbert), retired Chairman of the Royal Commission on Trade Unions and Employers' Associations, 1967–68, 21 July 1969.

Feather, Lord, General Secretary, TUC, 26 August 1969.

Foggon, George, Overseas Labour Adviser, Foreign and Commonwealth Office, 2 August 1975.

Gray, Hugh, Member of Parliament, 8 July 1969.

Greene, Lord, former General Secretary, National Union of Railwaymen; Chairman, TUC Economic Committee; member, TUC General Council: 24 July 1969, 4 August 1972, 31 July 1973.

Hartley, Andrew, Deputy Director, EEC Office (London), 23 July 1975, 9 August 1977, 12 August 1977, etc.

Haggan, D. E., Deputy Secretary, National Industrial Relations Court, 3 August 1972.

Heath, Edward, former Prime Minister, 13 April 1978.

Hurst, Harry, Deputy Overseas Labour Adviser, Foreign and Commonwealth Office, 12 August 1975.

Lea, David, Staff Member, TUC Economic Department, 10 July 1969 (now Assistant General Secretary of TUC).

Lilly, Peter, Chairman, Bow Group; Investment Analyst, several interviews, 1974–77.

Lloyd, Michael, European Communities Office (London), 20 July 1977.

Lowry, Patrick, Director, Industrial Relations, British Leyland, 8 August 1972.

Mackintosh, John P., Member of Parliament, November 1974, 20 July 1975, etc.

Macmillan, Maurice, former Minister of Labour, 16 August 1977.

Moore, A. B., Assistant Secretary, Department of Employment, 29 July 1975.

Mortimer, James, Chairman, Advisory and Conciliation Service; former member, National Board for Prices and Incomes, 5 August 1969, 1 August 1972, 19 July 1977.

Murray, Len, then Secretary, TUC Economic Department; now General Secretary, TUC: 31 July 1969.

Pendlebury, Rupert, Research Department, Amalgamated Union of Engineering Workers, 28 July 1972.

Pinder, John, Director, Political and Economic Planning, 28 July 1975.

Prentice, Reginald, Member of Parliament; former spokesman, Industrial Relations, Labour Party, 24 July 1972.

Roberts, Prof. B. C., London School of Economics and Political Science, 17 August 1972.

Scott, Nicholas, Member of Parliament, 26 July 1972.

Shanks, Michael, author; Director, BOC International; former Director-General, Social Affairs, EEC: 25 July 1969, 26 July 1972, 3 August 1977.

Silkin, John, Minister, Ministry of Agriculture, 15 August 1977.

Smith, Edward, Cabinet Office, 28 July 1975.

Swindon, Alan, Director, Industrial Relations, Confederation of British Industry, November 1974, 13 August 1975, 17 August 1977, etc.

Teague, Michael, Research Department, Association of Scientific, Technical and Managerial Staffs, 2 August 1972.

Torode, John, former Labour Correspondent, *Guardian*, 23 August 1972.

Urwin, D. H., Deputy General Secretary, Transport and General Workers Union; member, TUC General Council: 2 August 1977.

Willis, Norman, Head of Research Department, Transport and General Workers Union; now Assistant General Secretary, TUC: 7 August 1972.

Woodcock, George, former General Secretary, TUC; former Chairman, Commission on Industrial Relations: 12 July 1969, 26 July 1972, 21 August 1972, 26 July 1973.

Plus other members of the TUC staff, union leaders, politicians and civil servants who wish to remain anonymous.

Index

Compiled by Ann P. Barham

Note: Alphabetical arrangement is word by word; abbreviations (CBI, TUC etc.) are at the beginning of the appropriate letter sequence.

TUC (*contd.*)

government support for European proposals, 150, 151–2, 153, 155–6

Heath's letter to on Relativities report, 101

Heath's mistrust of, 100

Heath urges into talks with government, 78–9

informal meetings with Labour ministers, 27

initiative on voluntary reform, 36–9

meeting with Harold Wilson (11 Apr. 1969), 33–4

meetings with Anthony Barber and Robert Carr (Aug.–Sep. 1970), 68

NEDC members meet with Dennis Healey, 128

negative power of, 6, 66–7, 107, 134

non-cooperation with Conservatives, 54, 55–8

Programme for Action, 36–9, 40–1

relationship with Labour Party through Liason Committee, 108–12

renewed talks with Conservative Government (Summer 1973), 91–3

representation in Europe (*see also* ETUC), 6–7, 134–56

contact through EEC Commissioners, 144

ETUC, 138–9, 146–9, 153, 155, 156

ESC, 140–2, 149–52, 153, 154, 155

other committees, 143–4

policy goals, 136–7

problem of policy implementation, 152–6

role in economic decision-making, 2

in Liaison Committee, 110–13

under Conservatives, 66–7, 76, 78–86, 104

under Labour, 106–7, 116–21, 123

role in miners' dispute, 97–102, 103–4

Rule 11, 38, 42–4, 47–8

Special Congresses:

5 June 1969, 39, 40–1

18 Mar. 1971, 55–7

Mar. 1973, 88–9

16 June, 1976, 124–5

special relationship with Labour governments, 4, 8, 16–17, 23, 27, 132, 156

talks with Conservative Government and CBI through NEDC, 73–6, 79–86

traditional relationship with Conservatives, 3, 9, 50–1, 69, 93, 103–5, 156

effect of cooperation on internal union politics, 79, 81, 84–5, 104–5

TUC General Council:

concern at operation of social contract, 129–30

conflict within, 55, 56–7, 79–80

conflicting pressures on, 114–15

determination to resist industrial relations legislation, 15–17, 22–3, 24

discussion on future of social contract, 118–19

Finance and General Purposes Committee, 23–4, 61–2

meeting with Edward Heath and senior ministers (11 Mar. 1971), 72–3

meeting with Robert Carr and Sir Geoffrey Howe (18 Oct. 1970), 54

meetings with Barbara Castle (1968–9), 17–18, 23–4, 37–8, 38–9

meetings with Harold Wilson and Barbara Castle (May–June 1969), 37–8, 38–9, 41–2, 43–4, 46–8

opposition to penal sanctions, 38–9, 44

plans for general strike (1972), 62–3 strike averted, 64

public campaign against industrial relations legislation, 54–5

recommends one-day national strike (1973), 89